Praise for Kay Mehl Miller's
Living With the Stranger in Me:
An Exploration of Aging

Don't get a facelift. Get a life-lift with this scintillating journey to a new you. You'll laugh, you'll cry, you'll find surprising revelations as you discover that it is possible to age with panache and joie de vivre.

—**MARY McELROY, playwright and educator**

In her new book, Kay Mehl Miller spins a tale of nothing more or less important than rediscovering life and how to live it after confronting loss and the knowledge of her own mortality. In a narrative that runs from the confines of her kitchen to the piazzas of Italy we are privileged to watch each awakening, each rediscovery of what it means to be alive and human, both the good and the bad. A testament to the power of life to not just endure, but also to thrive; this is a deeply moving book for all who do not wish their later years to be merely "twilight."

—**THE REV. R. TIMOTHY CARNAHAN,**
Pastor, Faith Lutheran Church

An engaging journey of love, loss, aging and discovery of self, Kay Mehl Miller's *Living with the Stranger in Me* is a story to which we who age relate. With the death of her longtime spouse, a devastated Kay is alienated from life. She confronts the unwelcome stranger living within her through looking for spiritual solace, traveling, and writing her way back with compassion, insight, and humor.

—KAREN BATCHELOR, educator and author of textbooks, award-winning poems and short stories and the novel *Murder at Ocean View College*

In her latest book Kay Mehl Miller confronts the fearful struggles of old age, using the unique perspective of her own life experiences to provide lessons for making these latter years full and satisfying.

—BOB WARDEN, Publisher, *Word & Quill Press*

LIVING WITH THE STRANGER IN ME

An Exploration of Aging

KAY MEHL MILLER PH.D.

Living With the Stranger in Me: An Exploration of Aging

ISBN: 1463556888

ISBN: 9781463556884

kaymill@aol.com

Author's photo
Jonathan Hayden

Printed in the United States of America
First Printing 2011

Address all inquiries to:
kaymill@aol.com
(707) 537-0139

Living With the Stranger in Me: An Exploration of Aging/
Kay Mehl Miller, Ph.D.

1. Aging 2. Grief 3. Women's Issues 4. Non-fiction

For my sisters Marion and Flo. All these years we've taught, fought, and loved one another. And for Steve whose filial devotion sustains me.

Acknowledgments

Vera Abramo laughed with enjoyment, when I read to her the essay which introduces the stranger in me, and then she insisted I write a book on aging.

I brought each newborn chapter to my weekly women's group whose members made comments critical to the book's development. Myra Kramer, Anne Lebowitz, Maureen Rumford, and Helga Spizman, avid readers all, kept me focused and challenged me to remain open and honest in telling my story.

Karen Batchelor, my editor, spent many hours assisting me in the professional development of my work. Mary McElroy prodded me to stay aware of the needs of my audience, bringing new creative energy and boldness to my work. Members of my Redwood Writers critique group, especially Osha Hayden and her husband Jonathan, were particularly helpful to me in making decisions on the preface, introduction, and back cover material.

As the publication deadline neared, Bob Warden, who had nurtured me through the publication of my first book, read the new manuscript and spent many hours in helping me polish it. His professional experience was invaluable.

Finally, it was my pastor Tim Carnahan who led me back to writing itself when my confidence in myself needed a boost. The story is in the pages that follow. My deepest thanks to all.

Contents

Preface

Go ahead, take a peek. You know you want to. Go on. Do it. Aging isn't catching, just inevitable. If we are lucky, we do get old, and, if we face certain truths and overcome our fears, we can actually enjoy aging. Aging, after all, is the normal response to living life one day at a time.

Oh, I know you don't want to age. Neither did I, but here I am, already well into my seventies and, yet, in my head and my heart, I am no more than an active thirty-something. You see, there are pleasant surprises to aging. For instance, I have discovered that as long as I am reasonably healthy, I am ageless! There are even times when I actually forget how old I am. (Old-age forgetfulness does have its advantages!)

I have lost my youth. So what! There has never been a loss for me without a gain left in its stead. To age is to lose. There's no getting around that fact. Our looks, our figures, our roles in life, or, more seriously, our loved ones are all lost as a result of our aging.

To find the gain in the loss that comes with aging is sometimes challenging, a little like the small boy willingly shoveling manure out of the barn because he knows there's a pony in there somewhere.

My gain, as I move out of middle age (note that I still think of myself as middle-aged) and into the territory of old age, is that I am delightfully discovering that I am still a person with a lot more to contribute to life, a lot more to learn, and a lot more for which to be grateful. My spirits are high. My expectations of myself are realistic. I have found hope and confidence in a renewed spirituality.

Part of this gain was earned by having the courage to accept myself as a grieving person. No, I am not wearing a black dress and veil because my spouse died. Even though I keenly feel the loss of John, I have found that the need to survive that loss and to live productively while I still breathe is remarkably strong.

We don't easily talk about death. We shy away from grieving and even from those who grieve. Yet death comes, leaving survivors shocked, bereft, and, if the loss is great, intensely grieved. Grief had, and still has, much to teach me. Grieving has shown me the depth of sorrow, but also the endless depth of love, that I have within me. That love sustains me and puts into perspective difficulties that come with living.

In this book I share personal experiences I've had as an aging woman and insights these experiences have given me. I start with, an essay on menopause I wrote sometime in my fifties. *Being an Older Woman* is an audacious piece of writing that still makes me laugh. A second essay, *The Stranger in Me,* uses humor, as well, to explore the invisibility that older women experience. I wrote that essay when I was 65. It lay dormant in my computer for nearly ten years. After John died, I found the piece and shared it with my neighbor. Vera chortled all the way through it and declared,

"You have to make a book out of this!" That notion was the impetus for this book.

After the two essays the narrative of my experiences becomes introspective and insightful. Because the narrative is not strictly chronological, I have inserted a year in all the chapter titles, except the first one, to give a guide to the time events happened.

If I seem to wander, at times, in the territory of old age, remember: life is not lived in a straight line, nor in neat circles that meet our expectations of closure. Life moves on its own terms, sometimes diving into the past for a tool to illuminate the present or drifting away in reverie over an imagined future, as do I.

In sharing my experiences, I hope that others can readily identify and clearly see that aging can be a liberating and interesting stage of life. The key to successful aging, for me, is to participate in the process rather than fight it.

Introduction

When I began writing this book, I imagined aged widows reading it, for I wrote from the perspective of being newly widowed. However, as I told my story, I began to realize I was writing about a universal concern, aging; I had a larger audience to address.

My thoughts moved to addressing this larger audience. Most people, it seems, begin to fret about aging about the age of fifty, so that's where I began. The issues of aging were familiar to me, and, so, I wrote for an audience that was aging in ways similar to mine. As I began sharing the manuscript, younger readers gave me a new idea: this book, it seems, was a help to them in understanding their aging parents.

I realized then that as great as the jolt is of recognizing of our own aging, seeing aging in those we love can be a greater shock. Significant loved ones, especially parents, seem to decline at such inconvenient times in our lives, times when we are raising our own families or making our own retirement journeys. That happened to me, but I was fortunate enough to have two sisters who took care of our parents while our father was alive and, later, shared with me in taking care of our widowed mother.

We want to deny such aging, not only to keep our loved ones with us longer, but, to ward off the inevitable responsibility of caregiving. Making uncomfortable decisions for people who once were as powerful as God to us is daunting and can leave us feeling guilty over our own uncertainty, angry at being forced into such a bind, and ashamed for having such feelings.

My hope is that this book will help both types of readers: those who fret about their own aging and younger adults who seek an understanding of the challenges faced by their aging loved ones. Knowledge is power. With understanding, issues in aging, seen as problems, may be transformed, under the best of outcomes, to manageable events, preserving dignity and love, or, at the very least, make problems of aging less burdensome.

Chapter One:
An Older Woman

"*I* am an older woman. I *am* an older woman. I am an *older* woman." The mantra is I, day in, day out, striving to understand, striving to accept, striving to learn to become an older woman.

Thus begins an essay I wrote in 1993, when, looking at the approach of age 60, I begin to seriously fear aging. This lengthy essay continues:

Ye gods or goddesses! How did I get here? I am at age 59 suddenly very aware of myself. It's almost as if I am abruptly cast on shore to deal with myself as myself after years of drifting alone on a vast ocean while someone who said she was I was busy with the roles I played in life.

Of course, in reality, it was I, who followed a course in life as others do; for me: childhood, school, marriage, children, teaching, divorce, remarriage, running my own business, another divorce, new relationship, moving, and, finally, a stopping place. Now, simply being, or I should say *learning to be*, eclipses the doing. For I am not only older in this stage of life, but I am finding that I need to know the essential in me, the part of me that survived the roles.

My first sign that I am really older was being fatter. Suddenly this body of mine, which had gone through its periods of lean and fat before, ballooned. I popped out in droopy flesh at alarming rates and couldn't seem to help myself. I knew that life was changing drastically for me when I began to grow so very rapidly. As the pounds rolled in daily on the scale, I had the distinct sense that my body was trying to protect me by covering me up, preserving an inner self in danger of being lost. If I had not gained weight and been focused on and alarmed by the gain, perhaps I would have become very depressed at losing my place in life—no more being mother, teacher, student, counselor.

I could not completely validate this justification for being fat. Although it made sense that I did need protection from loss, in my mind lived too many critical voices that, over the years, spoke of lack of self-control as the reason for obesity. Surely, the way my life was out of control gave credence to that rationalization.

Nevertheless, I tried to validate my experiences, my theories, and my fears by talking to others. I wanted to be heard, but instead, I got advice. The doctor said, "Lose weight." My partner said, "Stop being depressed." My older sister said, "Cheer up." My younger said, "You should have my problems." No one said, "I know. I've been there," except, maybe, my best friend Ann, thousands of miles away and in the midst of her own crises. Her soft, sympathetic murmurs of "aw" did help and so did her willingness to listen, but I needed more. Yet, more was not within my grasp for a long, long time.

As the pounds piled on, I began to lose my libido. With a growing panic, I noticed that my physical sex was atrophying. My vagina seemed to be folding into itself, the clitoris shrinking and withdrawing even its hood into itself, the labia thinning and lifeless, the vagina walls dry. To add insult to injury, my pubis began to bald and the few remaining traces of hair became beard-like. It was a nightmare.

I ran to the doctor, and he said, "Estrogen." I said, "No." I had researched and studied long for this moment, and I knew what estrogen had done to the menopausal women of the 60's who were to be "forever young." Cancer grew in those who took unopposed estrogen. Of course, this doctor, and another doctor, and even a third doctor all said, "It's safer now. Progestin has been added. Besides, you'll protect your heart. The benefits outweigh the risks." Not in my book. My big breasts had ached, in their prime, with fibrous cysts and I was not about to deliberately feed them estrogen, opposed or not. When I would not listen to them, the doctors shook their heads, one almost angrily rebuking, "If you were my wife, you would be on estrogen replacement therapy."

Well, I wouldn't allow estrogen replacement therapy, and since I was offered no other therapy, but the door, I walked out of the doctors' offices. I clearly got the message. I was an "uppity" woman sentenced to shunning by the medical profession.

Once, in a weak and desperate moment, I returned to one of the doctors, begging for a physical exam. I was so ashamed of my body, so afraid of the changes that were happening. Even though I had read, and read, and read about menopause, the reality was something I hadn't expected. I had had a hysterectomy at 35. I knew there would be no cessation of bleeding, no irregular patterns, to mark the passage for me. My ovaries were intact and served me well during the years between hysterectomy and menopause.

I was at the doctor's because my massage therapist had a premonition of something wrong with my breasts (they were growing), and she begged me to get a mammogram (which my doctor refused because it hadn't been a year since the

3

last one). I wanted a physical exam for reassurance, but the doctor said no—the insurance wouldn't pay for a physical and he wasn't going to give me a freebie. When I asked what a physical exam would cost, he didn't answer the question, and said, instead, he didn't have time and I should "lose some weight." I burst into tears. I couldn't help it. I was so vulnerable at that point. He looked at me for a moment, a look I felt rather than saw since my head was down. Then, abruptly, he left the room. I cried long enough and loud enough, I think now, for someone to hear. I wasn't seeking sympathy or attention at this point; I was just too full of despair to hold in my grief. No one came. Finally, I put on my coat, and left his office, never to return.

I should say that the doctors I've mentioned did not know me. I had moved to their area earlier that year, and I was in personal crises while trying to find a permanent doctor. These medical men had no idea who I was other than I was a newly degreed Ph.D. (whom they called "Mrs."). They did not seem to want to get acquainted, and, indeed, were upset, themselves, since HMOs were just beginning to threaten private practices and they had not yet worked out their part of this new turf.

I went home depressed and stayed depressed. The rain relentlessly belting Northern California that winter, day after day, with no letup in the perpetual gray dreariness of days and the cold wet darkness of night, deepened my misery. After 23 years of living in the sunshine of Hawaii, I had no defense against the unremitting assault of flat-out cold and gloomy weather.

Yet, there is in me an inner strength that always comes to act for me when I cannot consciously act on my own. This spirit within wants life for me. There was a gentle nagging to "do something," and so I chose to read. John, my partner, bought for me Gail Sheehy's *The Silent Passage: Menopause.* The book comforted me though it didn't solve my problems. Another book, Susun Weed's *Menopausal Years* gave me practical advice, but I was daunted by the truly awesome power in entering the realm of the Goddess with its herbal remedies and self-loving rituals. Even though I am a feminist, I am also a child of the patriarchy imbued with the insensible fear taught by *that* awesome power, and though attracted by the Goddess, I was also intimidated by the possibility of being riveted into yet another confining and ruinous belief system. I had, and still have, a trust problem with any systematic explanation of the mysterious in life. Not that I don't believe in the mysterious. I do. Another of my resources, an unknown intuitive force that seems to operate as a life guide for me is mysterious. I've heard this particular mystery called *serendipity* by those who are accepting of its marvels and *coincidence* by cynics who dismiss its existence. Whatever it is, the manifestation of its works, in this instance, was a notice for a Saturday workshop on menopause.

I came from that workshop with a beginning knowledge of herbs and a feeling of camaraderie with the women who attended, some comfortable with the Goddess and her rituals, some not. We were all united in our interest in menopause, our experiences with a less than understanding medical profession, and our determination to share and learn more about our own bodies and health.

Still, I resisted treating myself until Cathy, John's daughter, came to visit and urged me to try wild yam root. I had not bought or used the expensive creams with wild yam root that had been touted in the workshop. Cathy came with the wild yam root in a powered state, which she had put into capsules herself. I swallowed two. The effect was nearly immediate. I felt something, a heightened awareness, a lessening of the aches and pains of what I had thought was the beginning of arthritis. When Cathy left, I went to the health store, bought a dollar's worth of wild yam root powder and some gelatin capsules and made some capsules of my own.

After a week or so of taking the capsules, I noticed that my vagina felt less dry. As time went on, the labia started to become thick again and my pubic area began to plump out. Some soft hair returned, not much, but the stubble was gone. I began to take the wild yam root, a capsule a day for 28 days, none for seven days, and then the one capsule dose on a cycle of 28 days again. After a year of following this schedule, I feel whole again. Not young, not restored to the hot sexiness of youth, but whole, able to enjoy being sexual again, able to feel more in control of myself—the unspeakable ravages reversed to a manageable and dignified aging.

I learned something with that long, hurtful at times, but, ultimately, enlightening experience of dealing with the issues of menopause. The only way to achieve satisfaction for myself is for me to take charge, to forget the experts and trust myself in finding my own way to wholeness. I've learned this before and probably shall learn it again. I cannot entirely fight the years of indoctrination. For me, being a woman still means a return to that dependence on the wisdom of others that I was taught as a child, even when that dependence fails me, for I have been inculcated with the established ways of the world and have felt the punishments for not finding my place and keeping it. Yet, I cannot continue in the old ways either for they are unhealthy for me. The reality of being a woman for me, then, is discovering and validating my own independence for this is the path to life and meaning. The confusion and despair, I feel, in being independent is my own longing for connection and acceptance. I have to work hard to have both independence and connection. When it all develops and gels, a certain peace and perfection is attained, and being an independent woman brings confidence and joy.

And so the essay ends, *and I ask myself what does a 59-year-old woman in 1993 know about aging?* Plenty, perhaps, but there was so much more for me to learn than when I wrote that essay on being an older woman.

In my forty-ninth year, about the first quarter of 1984, I began to worry about turning fifty. A tiny twinge of fear nagged me for I became conscious, really conscious for the first time in my life, of my mortality. Fifty is half a century! A century is a hundred years and few people live to see a hundred. I had already lived the better half of that century, hadn't I? Aging baby boomers deflect this same reasoning by declaring fifty "the new thirty." We wish, don't we? No, fifty is a distinct marker of an inescapable decline, one that, in my forty-ninth year, chilled me in its implication. We are, after all, finite creatures.

How we age without fear becomes a question far too relevant to contemplate. When that strange creature, age, comes to live within us, our first instinct is to deny that we are or will ever become old. I still feel that way at seventy-five, and I'm pretty sure that this attitude is basically a healthy one. After all, as long as we are alive we need to feel and act alive. We can't appreciate much about life if we allow fear to dominate our thoughts, attitudes, and actions.

I turned fifty in August of 1984, just a couple of months after my son Steve came out to me as gay and shook my certainty to the core. I also graduated from the University of Hawaii that August with a Master of Education Degree, specializing in community counseling.

The fact that I was just getting around to earning an advanced degree, while exhilarating in its accomplishment, felt a bit shameful; fifty seemed old for new beginnings. Graduate degrees were for the young who had time and energy to build careers. What was I thinking? I had no idea that sunny day that many new beginnings were in store for me as I aged.

A year after I graduated, my mother died, and just ten months later Edna died as well. Edna was my first cousin, married to John, who in the fourth month of his grief sought me out, a story that unfolds later in this book. John was a major new beginning for me.

Physically, my body was aging. I'm not sure when I became aware of my menopause for I had had a hysterectomy at thirty-five, precluding certain signals women get that they are in menopause. Maybe I just didn't have the time to think about menopause, as life in my fifties expanded. Once I got used to having a gay son, I began writing columns on gay and lesbian issues. I started my own psychotherapy business, seeing clients in my home, and worked with abused women at the Family Peace Center. I also helped my college mentor design classes in understanding alcoholism for his graduate counseling students, and, when John came to live with me, I helped him by typing and editing his short stories and his first book.

Everything came to a screeching halt when John and I decided to move to California in 1992, the year I graduated with my doctorate from Saybrook University in San Francisco.

Settling down in 1993 in an active adult community, I lived among seniors who were mostly older than I in a community that restricted me from starting a business in my home and in a mainland town that seemed very foreign after living for twenty-three years in multi-cultural Hawaii.

I felt old. I felt useless. Often when I feel something intensely, I write. Sometime that year I wrote the essay describing my feelings on being an older woman and left it on my computer for me to find years later.

When I finished the essay, I laid aside my writing and turned toward my new life. I became president of the community's swim club and we joined the New Yorkers Club and began to partake of some of the activities of our golden ghetto, the senior community designed for those over fifty-five.

When sixty rolled around, I was in a better frame of mind, having survived my fifties without the imagined decline except for the "change of life" issues that decade brought. Sixty, for me, was virtuous because it promised a bit of security with retirement benefits from the federal government. Sixty was also problematic for I was living with a man who was twenty-three years my senior and showing signs of wearing out. I wasn't quite sure what I wanted. I knew I didn't want a full-time caregiver role, but John needed my care and I loved him. Our commitment to one another as registered domestic partners had the "better or worse" aspect of marriage; I assumed the role of caregiver.

In my seventies the "worse" happened. John died. I was thrust into an upheaval I had not expected. What I didn't know about mourning, I learned, and not in a hurry either. The darkness I experienced was not so much an event of grief over a lost loved one, as it was grief and confusion over the loss of my own life; the life that had become familiar and comforting was gone. Now what?

Chapter Two:
Suddenly Single
(2009)

There's a largely unconscious and seldom appreciated security in having someone who loves you by your side daily. Jokes are made about the partner to whom you made a commitment for life, but not for lunch. A partner underfoot is sometimes an impediment to life's enjoyment for his or her needs have to be considered before one can blithefully make a luncheon date with a friend—"you're sure you don't mind. I'll be back by two, two-thirty at the latest. I left a peanut butter and jelly sandwich in the fridge for you."

Ours was a May-December romance of the late May-December variety. John was 75 and I, 52, when we partnered. Surprisingly, there was a lot of life left for enjoyable togetherness; John died in 2007, the day after his 96th birthday.

Six months later, while idly reviewing files in my computer, I came upon *The Stranger in Me*, another essay—this one written when I was 65. I was struck by the idea that the essay's theme of restiveness and searching for something beyond ordinary satisfaction with one's life is universal, a condition that becomes particularly insistent as one ages. This essay was related to the earlier one *Being an Older Woman,* but was more reflective. What struck me as awesome, however, was that the feelings and concerns about aging I had at 65 were still relevant ten years later. I'm not sure what I expected of aging even with the example provided by watching John live into his nineties. Old age is always a future event, but the mind tends to store fearful societal images, which, for the most part, are overflowing with ridicule and contempt. We hear the words *old geezer* or *old hag.* At best, when we think of *old, as* in *grandparents,* there is fond nostalgia at lives perhaps well-lived, but definitely, nearly over. The usefulness of our elders lies in drawing wisdom from the past for us, seasoned advice which we generally ignore. John's dying changed me; for while he lived, I was the youngster; with him gone, my future had arrived.

Finding the essay made me pensive. The death of my beloved partner left me in a strange place. I knew I would grieve. When you lose someone you love, you grieve, but I never expected I would feel an even more urgent loss, one that would challenge me as much or more than I've ever been challenged. I lost my bearings. I didn't know who I was or what to do with myself.

I felt eerily detached from life and angry. I wondered how much life is left when one is in her seventies. Losses threatened to overwhelm me. I felt sorry for myself. I had no work at that point. I had no community—or so I thought. To take care of John I had given up work with the gay community and writing a monthly column for their news outlets. That world moved on without me. I had family, but the members of one's family have lives of their own without room for the drab life I imagined for myself now. Although I functioned in taking basic care of myself, I didn't know or even like the self I had suddenly become.

I was single again, single in my seventies! Is my life extraneous without a partner? Is it rich in memories of past glories, but poor in prospect for worthwhile future achievements? I was no longer someone's spouse, no longer a helpmate, no longer intimately connected to another human being. I had a different status, which, to me, amounted to no status at all.

This phase of grieving is so painful. Had I stayed in my self-pitying attitude, I'm sure I would have sickened and died.

All the attendant problems that being single brings were mine once more, an unwelcome presence in my late stage in life. All the feelings these problems generate came back in uncomfortable and sometimes embarrassing detail. At times I felt as if I were going crazy, so foreign to me was my new position in life. Unexpectedly, in a quiet moment of reflection I gained some clarity and, with it, a glimmer of hope: I would have to rebuild my life, even though I had no clue on how to do this.

The rebuilding of my life began with a stained glass window in a church that I decided on impulse to visit. The light streaming through that window calmed and comforted me. I don't particularly like religion; so to go to church was a radical act on my part. I kept coming back to that window, that light that beckoned me. I didn't realize it then, but this was the beginning of an engagement with a spirituality that gave me a new perspective on aging and led me back to feeling truly alive again, my fears of aging gone, and my trust in sufficiency restored.

Getting there involved work, putting one foot in front of the other without really knowing where I was going until I got there. Most of the time I felt like a stranger had taken my place in the world. When I found in my computer the essay I had written much earlier, I was intrigued; I had felt a stranger in me before! Here is that essay, written in 1999 when John was still with me.

The Stranger in Me

This is a strange place to be—this being old. I don't honestly know how I got here. Sure, there are markers as we age, but being old is in the future. Even now, I am among the young-old, having passed only my 65th birthday, so I can fudge on the being old business, can't I?

I live in a community for active adults, a euphemism for senior citizens, which is, of course, another euphemism for old people.

I play with words trying to get used to the idea of age as in *old, really* old.

The bright Baby Boomers, my own son being among them, tell me that being old is not really a state of being. As long as I am active and independent, why, then I am not among the old no matter what the calendar says! When a person is ill and becomes dependent on others, *then* that person is old. Time enough, then, to be old when I lose my health. Not now. Please, not now.

I look to television to see the role models of old people. Why, there we are bicycling down hills, hugging grandchildren, making meals for families that come home, and, yes, taking vitamins, checking our blood pressure or planning our next cruise—although fewer of us are doing that in television commercials since the youngsters have discovered cruising Disney-style with their parents.

My mail thinks I'm old. How many times was I warned before my 65th birthday that I'd better sign up for life insurance before it is too late? Having missed the deadline for life insurance, I am now inundated with dire warnings that I had better buy long-term care insurance. Once in awhile I am offered a cemetery plot or a prepaid funeral. My wastebasket runneth over.

Congress passed and the President signed a legal provision that should I want to go to work, I will no longer lose a dollar in Social Security benefits for every two I make over a certain basic amount, so I could go back to work. Problem is that I have overeducated myself. With a doctorate in psychology, I really don't want to drive a taxi, but then neither do I want to go to work for younger people still discovering their skills. I can be a formidable presence with my knowledge and experience. I missed my time to be the boss and am now too qualified to be an employee.

How did I learn this? By volunteering. The young therapists, who run wonderful programs that help people, trained me in their methods, but I was never comfortable doing things their way. I wanted to lead them instead of following their lead. Age gave me the wisdom not to instruct them. Trying to change the programs they had formed with their hearts and souls would have been egotistical indeed! I craved an active creative role, so I stopped volunteering.

There are some saintly elders who *do* volunteer and are perfectly happy having someone else make the policies. I envy them. They have mastered the art of the possible, gaining enjoyment from being useful without having to be in charge.

When I find a cause about which I am passionate, I can find a niche as head of a committee to educate others about the cause, and I am happy with such work. Usually, these efforts are short-lived as, for instance, an election settles the issue, and I am, once more, at loose ends.

No, the time has passed, for me, to be active in the working world. I can, and I do, write, including a monthly column for which I am paid, but I am not widely published. I have written a book about the columns and my personal story around the issues the columns reflect.

I have a family, a partner with whom I am close and relatives on his side, including grandchildren and a great-grandchild. I have a son with a partner, both of whom I adore. Another son is estranged from me so I don't get to interact with my two grandchildren, a not uncommon phenomenon among my generation. While other women my age tell stories about their wonderful grandchildren, I am gracious in listening without too much comment, lest my own hurt intrude on their happy state. I am glad for them, and I actively work at not feeling sorry for myself. After all, I did raise that son to be independent, and I hope he and his family are living a full and satisfying life.

Looking at the events in my life, you could say I have a life. What's the complaint? Why do I feel like such a stranger to myself? Because being in this stage of life *is* strange. There are no role models for me or other women my age. Our mothers were of a different time, a time when women stayed home to raise their children, and, then, at retirement age, if they were lucky, traveled or, at least, spent winters in the sun before getting so old that they returned home for a few years with family before dying.

My generation was referred to as a *lost generation*, an echo of the better-known Lost Generation of the 1920s. Our prime was in the 1950's, that historical period when the world was rebuilding itself after World War II and scaring itself with worry over a nuclear holocaust. We were the first children to "duck and cover" under our school desks, believing our practiced response would save us, even as we read of people purchasing concrete bomb shelters, hoping to keep out the deadly radiation. We were naive. It took the Vietnam War to make cynics out of people, and while some of my generation moved in that direction, I never can quite let go of the hope that the nation that protected and nurtured me as a child will re-emerge.

We gave our children all the gifts of prosperity that were denied to us; we had little during the Depression years and had to sacrifice during the war years. By the 1960s, women became more powerful, so as a young mother, I was able to work on a career. I wanted to write novels, yet with family responsibilities, I couldn't get the writing career going; I ended up teaching English to junior high youngsters. I put my own dreams on hold to provide for my family. When my sons grew up, properly educated, and ready for the world, it felt too late for me.

Not that I didn't try. I pursued and won both a master's degree and a doctorate. By the time I finished, I was 58, more ready for retirement than the challenge of competing for a psychologist's license and building a practice of my own. Besides, once again, I made a commitment to a partner, and I needed to take into consideration what kind of life I wanted with him. In the end, I opted for time with him, rather than a risky gamble at beginning a career in my sixties.

The pattern for me is obvious. Although I reach for my own fulfillment, my fulfillment is not just in self-improvement; it is also in being in a relationship.

Yet, knowing this is not enough. There is within me a restlessness that leads to days of depression. Some would say that I need a spiritual program for self-fulfillment, and they just may be right. Yet, I've done that. I've been involved in church and in psychological journeys, and always the involvement is satisfying for a finite time, and, then, something happens to move me away. Perhaps it's my questioning nature, a feeling that the answers offered me are based on motives that are less than pure. If I support a certain religion, I cannot support women who need to be free to make a choice on abortion or men and women who are discriminated against because they are perceived to make a choice, rather than viewed as biologically made as gay, lesbian, bisexual, or transgender. If I choose a religion or psychological path that is inclusive, invariably I find something missing. Maybe an intellectual approach negates the mystery and awe I crave. Sometimes, I feel that a guru is the one worshiped, and he simply is not large enough for me. Putting my trust in a goddess is appealing, but then I feel that my position will be one as crone, vessel of wisdom and precursor to death. My soul is chilled by the prospect. Old women are not yet wise in our society; otherwise, we would be revered in all our infinite variety, rather than so narrowly defined.

I am not large enough myself to create my own god. Not that I don't try. The effort pays off on sleepless nights when I "turn over" my restlessness to a power that sustains me. That's the closest I get, and I'm really grateful for that small connection.

I do like the outdoors. The sea has always been balm to me, and, perhaps, had I been a fish, I would have lived in ecstasy until caught and eaten but, who knows, maybe fish, too, are restless when they are older and wiser. The warmth of the sun, the green of the land, the magnificence of hills, the reach of trees, and the blue of the sky dotted with gliding birds provide my strongest connection to an eternal satisfaction.

So, I wonder about the stranger within me. This being, who has accomplished goals and has health and wealth enough to be fine at the moment, has lost her momentum, her zest for life, even, to some extent, the anger that lights passion and sparks action. It's as if I have done what I was supposed to do and am now asked to learn how to simply be.

When I was a schoolgirl, learning my verbs, I pondered over the infinitive "to be," which was described as a "state of existence." I had to take that phrase on faith, because, being young, I didn't need assurance of existence. I was content with being. I was too intent on surviving the slings and arrows of growing up in a family that seemed in a perpetual feud over something. I was awed by nature and thrilled by books and learning. I looked forward to being grown and in charge of my own life. All the forms of the verb "to be" had modifiers—"intent on surviving," "awed," "thrilled," "grown." What modifiers have I now? "Old," of course, but, then, what does "old" mean?

I guess I really am in a "state of existence," just as befuddled by the phrase as I was when I was a schoolgirl.

The vision I have is that I will learn to live each day in the grace of being—being healthy, being fortunate and being loved, for I am all that. I will learn that a state without modifiers—a simple affirmation that "life is"—is sufficient. I hope I am lucky enough to learn I do not have to *be something* other than what I am in order to live and to enjoy my life.

Until then, I am a stranger to being old, but I am, I think, a friend to myself.

Chapter Three:
Strange Territory
(2009)

Ten years after writing *The Stranger in Me* I'm older in body, older in health issues, and in spirit seesawing between old and young. I'm still in the same active adult community, in the same house and still blessed with the same family, except, my mind keeps endlessly circling the same sad inescapable fact: John—the one who made all the difference, my closest friend and confidant, my mate of 20 years, the man I loved with my whole heart—has died.

There are long, soulful pauses as I write. The reality of losing John must sink in once again. For I am writing without him here to encourage me, to remind me of events that should be recorded, to sit back and take my pages in hand and solemnly read each word before offering advice. His critiques kept me focused. If I wandered, he'd show me where I should go with the next word, the next paragraph, the next chapter.

Where do I go from here, John? What do I do with my life without you?

The question isn't mine alone, nor is it relevant to old age only. With the loss of a loved one, life changes drastically for the one left behind. Old or young, the survivor is thrust into a new life, a life that has some familiarity, some connectedness to the life lived thus far, but a life that feels totally different.

Where do I go from here? I'm in strange territory indeed. In the beginning, I didn't know there were others like me, older women who had lost their spouses and were feeling as isolated as I was. The widows that I did know appeared already acclimated to their loss; they didn't talk about it. The ones I met in a grieving group seemed in a world of their own. I didn't feel close to them, nor they to me. Had I lost the ability to relate?

I felt old. Yes, finally, I can say "old," maybe not accept "old," but say it, yes. Living it? Well, that's a different story. No one wants to live old.

John used to say, "Never get old," and he said it almost up to the day he died at 96. I think he meant never give up on life until you have to.

When John died, grief made me feel old. Grief made me helpless. Grief brought depression to me. I'd go through the mechanics of life: eating, sleeping, and fulfilling obligations. Mostly, I played hours of games on the computer, eyes glued to the screen, body glued to the chair, switching from game to game without regard to winning or losing—anything to dull my senses, any mindless thing to avoid trying to untangle the mess made by being alone, really alone, for the first time in my life. My future had no possibilities or so I thought.

A month after John's death, I glanced at my calendar and saw the word "Sunday." I had been an infrequent churchgoer for most of my adult life, yet something made me write the word "church" in that Sunday's calendar space, and when Sunday came I went to church. The church I chose was one where John met with the Transitions group, a support group for older men sponsored by a community mental health association. I knew the church, too, from other organizations that met there so I was able to walk in as a stranger, but with some expectation of acceptance.

I didn't need conversion. I was already a child of God in my thinking and in practice. As a member of a twelve-step program, recovery from my addiction meant finding a power greater than myself and relying on that power. Working the program meant working with the God of my understanding and that God wasn't in a church. Somewhat akin to the experience I had with the grieving widows, I felt uncomfortable with the idea of looking for a connection with a community of believers. I wanted comfort, not ritual, not dogma. I wanted someplace to go where John might be, so, as unlikely as going to church was for me, I went to church.

Comfort I got. Inside the church, above the altar, was a stained-glass creation window. It was round and its shapes of colors reminded me of a rainbow. Through the rainbow shone the outdoors, a wintry light, since it was January when I first came to church. The light, soft as it was, seemed nevertheless to shine on me; I felt the blessed relief of quiet, of John in spirit touching me.

That tenuous connection was enough to bring me back, but more was offered. A woman in the church approached and asked if I played bridge. How unexpected, how incongruous in a place of worship—how God-given an offer since I love to play bridge! Bridge: a card game. Bridge: a link between distinct places. Bridge: a promise of connection. I said yes and on the way out hugged the pastor and told him "I am called to play bridge."

One nice aspect about age is that eccentricity is forgiven. Hugs are allowed and crazy talk is expected. The pastor, younger than my younger son, hugged me back and simply said, "Good!"

Still, I had to go home. At home there was that eerie silence that tends to sing in one's ears. At home were loneliness and dark settling in as evening approached. At home was the lurking depression ready to consume me. At home, too, was television with voices to break the eerie silence, lights to tame the darkness, but, still, nothing to quell the depression—except putting one foot in front of the other and forfeiting my despair to a broom, a washing machine or a bed in need of making. Bread I have, God. What you *can* give me are my daily chores.

How ironic that I was on a quest for answers when I didn't even know what the questions were! Grief does that to you. Grief either consumes you with sadness so deep you want to hide or prods you into action, no matter how premature or inappropriate. You can hide in sleep, food, or in a bottle. I preferred sleep. I loved to go to bed, close my eyes and be done with the day. I even hoped, sometimes, that another day would not interrupt my sleep; who wants to wake to sadness? Action beyond my daily chores and the long hard work of putting John's affairs to rest wasn't a choice. The weekly trip to church and the monthly bridge game were my only new actions. Funny how I couldn't see then that these actions were movements toward a new life.

What wasn't articulated in full to me was that I had to rebuild my life. I knew I had to grieve. Everybody grieves, but then, after grief wasn't it reasonable to assume that life resumes? What a shock it had been to find myself suddenly single. The world about me was full of couples, full of families, enjoying their lives, and here was I muddling around by myself, confused out of my mind about how to act as a woman in her seventies longing for some intimacy.

As grief subsided and ability to face each day surfaced, my longing for a companion became embarrassingly acute. I'd scrutinize men's faces looking for an invitation to ask for more than a pleasant hello. I'd chide myself for looking, but still I'd look again. It became an obsession, an obsession I wasn't able to give voice to yet.

I took a trip to the city with a small group in a mini-bus to have lunch and see a play. The pleasant looking man I passed on my way to my seat looked at me and I said hello. Before I had warmed my own seat, he seated himself beside me. For a moment I was heartened, thrilled that here was my new companion, someone my own age, someone alone as well. We exchanged pleasantries and almost immediately he began talking about himself. He talked and talked and talked. I tried to tell him a little of myself, but when I did, he was reminded of something else he wanted to tell me about himself.

Age has its compensations. Long experience with people gave me the wisdom to know that this man was not my designated companion. He was, I suppose, a good man and probably suitable to a woman more ready than I to cater to a man so full of himself. I may have been unfair to judge him on such a brief encounter for I also was needy and, given the chance, I might have talked and talked and talked myself.

I did consider a younger man, a man I knew who had lost his wife and, subsequently, was hurt when a girlfriend he had thought cherished him changed her mind and ended their relationship. I was wary though. I knew this man well enough that I could sense trouble in his need for control. He knew me well enough to keep me at a distance for he liked me and he wasn't ready for a new relationship. We went to lunch twice and to a couple of concerts with the understanding that we were friends, only I couldn't help but feel attracted to him and, he, somewhat to me, but not enough. I felt foolish. What in the world was I doing? We stopped trying to be something other than casual with one another.

Looking for a new relationship is so awkward! Yet, I had to give myself points for trying. Lonely people sometimes are too frightened to try. Rejection is a hard rebuke to forwardness. Embarrassment can lead to withdrawal and further isolation. Fortunately, I didn't do that for I had women friends to talk to.

Yet, still the urge to couple, to have a warm body near me, to have someone to share my daily life was so insistent that I turned to the Internet. Here I found an organization that asked me enough questions about myself to search for a man that would be suited to my needs.

It was fun to read the results of the personality test, especially the positive traits detected by my answers. I was fair, considerate, collaborative and responsive on the positive side. On the other hand, I was too rational in solving problems, which tended to make others, who expected rescue, to see me as unsympathetic; those who believe people should solve their own problems would see me as too soft.

The personality profile went on for seven pages measuring my agreeableness, my openness, my conscientiousness, and my extroversion. After the first few pages, I got bored with it all and filed it away. The profile was carefully crafted, designed so I would take offense at nothing but would step up to the plate and purchase the services of the matchmaking organization.

I bought nothing. The organization sent me email teasers, short descriptions of men who might be interesting to me. I was hopeful when two possibilities near my age showed up on my monitor. Okay, I thought, I'll choose this one, and when I made the click on the link, up came the cost for the privilege of communicating with the chosen one. Now, maybe I could swing the cost, although income can be a problem when a partner dies. However, I kept feeling a nagging prohibition against actually putting out money to talk to a man, so I'd let the opportunities slide by.

Finally, a truly interesting description of a man who was living in my area caught my eye; I paid to see his photograph. Alas, he had withdrawn from the program and his photo was no longer available. This frustration occurred several times, even when I checked out the prospect the second I got the email.

It is bad enough to be rejected by a living, breathing human, but to have a faceless corporation raise my hopes for a new companion and then dash them in a blunt statement—not even, "We are sorry, the man you are seeking has been disconnected," was agony.

I felt so vulnerable, so totally naked in my need for intimacy and furiously embarrassed that I had to look for love on the Internet. I called the company.

My voice was shaking, "It's because I'm 75, isn't it?"

"No, no," the young male voice on the phone assured me. "We have lots of clients who are in their seventies."

"Yeah, you do. Men!" I countered. "It's easier to find a partner for an older man than for an aged woman."

He waffled. "You know if you were to be a little more specific in your description of yourself," he said. "For instance, what is your religion?"

I hesitated and then told him I was a Lutheran.

"Okay," he was typing in this new information. "Now, then," he was about to ask a new question. I interrupted, near tears now and he could hear them in my voice.

"Never mind," just cancel my subscription. I could barely talk.

"Are you sure?"

"Yes."

"Just a minute, ma'am." He put me on hold. When he came back, it was with good news. "I talked to my supervisor. If you really want to cancel your subscription, I am authorized to delete the upcoming charges for the remaining months." This was a confirmation to me, not so much of the salesman's empathy, but of the difficulty it would pose for the company to find a match for me.

It was done. I felt better.

I obviously wasn't really looking for a new relationship. I was looking for an end to my loneliness, an end to the emptiness of being a single person, albeit with family and friends, but alone in the daily rhythm of life, fulfilling my needs on my own with scant satisfaction; for family and friends, as kind as they were, had lives of their own to tend. There wasn't time enough in the universe to mend mine.

Chapter Four:
Familiar Ground
(1973–2009)

Shock is a merciful gift. In the initial shock of losing John, I would sense him near me. When I woke, I'd reach toward his pillow, convinced he was quietly sleeping beside me. While walking through the first few days, I felt his presence. He was in the next room, getting coffee. Only he wasn't. He was sitting in his chair watching television right beside me. Only he wasn't. He was there, and he wasn't there. Gradually, the illusion faded and I was left with tears that brimmed, tears I fought to suppress. For hadn't I wanted his suffering to stop? Hadn't I prayed for him to die?

I didn't know then that I was moving through processes in grief, processes that take time, but, in time, would be less raw, less haunting. There was to be a life ahead of me, but, early on, I couldn't see it or really believe in it.

I kept seeing John as he declined during the last years of his life, how he lost, bit by bit, the independence he so prized. It wasn't a sudden illness that took him, but the slow inexorable wearing down of his body until it could no longer support life. I had so much more to do to take care of him then, tasks that took physical and mental strength and a willingness to confront unpleasant realities. My nursing skills, compassion and patience were fully tested as I learned to work with and for John. When the suffering became acute, I prayed that he would die for I knew that death was near and I didn't want him to hurt any longer.

So strong was the impact of these memories that for a long time there were no pleasant memories. Gradually I was able once again to review our story.

When John and I got together, I was 52 and he a youthful 75. Edna, his wife of 46 years died in July of 1986, and, four months later, in his grief and his great need for someone to be a caring companion, John came to me, a surrogate for Edna. As her cousin, I had been loyally available to him during her illness and death. Now the cousin part in the relationship no longer existed. As we stood in the baggage area of the Honolulu Airport, John looked at me and said softly, "So beautiful." I knew then I was in trouble.

I was on a rational pathway in life when a grieving John put a solid temptation in my way. My first instinct was to fend him off, get him onto a rational pathway of his own and be there as a close friend for him. That's all. I was busy. I had completed a master's degree in education with a specialty in community counseling and already had set up a private practice in my home. I was also in the midst of writing my dissertation for a doctorate in psychology, and I had plans. I wanted to finish the doctorate, do an internship in Hawaii and apply for licensing as a clinical psychologist.

Besides, I was married! To Ted.

Just when we think we have life under our control, events occur to upset the order we have created. My intuition told me that being around John without Edna would radically change my life. The "so-beautiful" at the baggage claim was my cue to put a brake on John's intentions even before he made them known, but I'm not a cold, calculating person and neither was John. I was embarrassed.

Technically, John was family since Edna was my cousin, but in reality we weren't related by blood. I didn't understand the depth of loneliness grief exacts after a long and successful marriage, and though I trusted John, I had no intention of developing an intimate relationship with him.

My own tangled history of passionate encounters, long since renounced, made me aware of the dangers of not listening to intuition, yet I thought, erroneously, I could control John's interest in me. I didn't even suspect the weight of my own interest in him as I ignored my intuition and walked out of the airport with John.

My mother died nearly a year earlier than Edna, so I, too, had issues with grief. Beyond my mother's death, my husband had grown distant and moody. Ted was ten years younger than I. I met him in an early meeting of my twelve-step program. He and I shared the same date of coming to the program, May 1, 1973, and we'd joke that we were twins. Soon we were going to meetings together. When I divorced my first husband, Ted moved in with me. Our shared interest in our recovery from our addictions was the glue in our relationship. After seven years of living together, we married almost on a whim—our good friends had a fancy wedding and Ted and I got caught up in the heady sensation of good will and romantic fantasy such occasions promise. Big mistake. Once plans were in the works for the wedding, I wouldn't back out. Ted had never had a fancy wedding—he had married his first wife at a justice of the peace. He was genuinely excited about the wedding and I wanted him to have that experience though the truth was I would have preferred no ceremony at all.

Our twelve-step program teaches us to be honest for good reason. Without honesty, we get ourselves into situations that affect not only our own well-being, but hurt others around us. Since I had lived with Ted for seven years, I convinced myself that nothing would be different when we married, but I was wrong. For me marriage was a trap.

In my first marriage I was a mother of two in her mid-twenties, far away from my family of origin, and left to handle family affairs on my own every time my husband, an aviator with the U.S. Navy, left for a six-month tour of sea duty or on a shorter training mission. Even when home, if the phone rang in the middle of the night and duty called, my naval aviator husband abandoned me. From my perspective, marriage was lonely work and sacrifice with few benefits. Drowning my woes in a bottle and trying to be a good Navy wife when I hated being so confined began my descent into alcoholism, a decline hastened by the liberal attitudes of drugs, booze, rock and roll and open marriages in the decades of the sixties and seventies. I was 38 when I walked into my first twelve-step meeting and 40 when I divorced that husband to become a civilian once more.

My marriage with Ted wasn't a bad one. He was a good provider. Further, he loved to cook and fed my sons and me well. When my mother moved in with us, he and she traded recipes, and he was very good to her. I was in my own world of schoolwork. Ted looked up to me; I became a role model to him. He enrolled in college for the first time, but college was not his forté although he did complete an associate's degree. The difference in ages, education and interests created a gap between us, which grew wider as I stepped further into the world of academia and away from twelve-step meetings and shared work. Ted showed his independence and his competency by building the first computer we owned. His day work, his meetings, and his computer became his life.

Although Ted taught me how to use the computer, he was very defensive about its use, hovering over me and nervously exhorting me not to use this or that command, as he was sure I'd cause his computer to crash. Somehow, this exercise became a metaphor for our marriage. I was moving away from him. He sensed it and became depressed. I recommended therapy for him, not us, for I feared being asked to make another marital sacrifice. I was immersed in my studies and truly happy to be on a self-fulfilling pathway, and I didn't want to be stopped.

Soon Ted was going places by himself. He traveled to a high school reunion in Chicago where he met with an old love. I felt relief, not anxiety. He denied intimacy with her, even when I knew he wasn't telling me the truth. At home he'd spend long hours on the computer; I was asleep when he'd finally come to bed. The marriage was in its last stages, yet we were holding on for financial and emotional security as many couples do. Divorce has a grief of its own, which I think is never fully appreciated by those who have never experienced a divorce. Not wanting to experience that grief again, it seemed more reasonable, to me, to carve separate lives under the same roof than bring the house down.

Then came John with his "so beautiful," in the Honolulu Airport. I was startled, befuddled by the implications of what I was hearing. Was this appropriate behavior from a man so recently bereaved? Had he come to Hawaii, not only to attend a lecture his son was giving at the university, but with ulterior motives, motives that involved me? I hastily shifted into counseling mode. I drove him home and we began a long series of talks about his grief, about what he should do with his life with Edna gone from him, and how to satisfy his physical needs. Being John's counselor was tricky. I could feel the tension between us. Even more alarming I could feel myself wanting to be involved. This was not only a man who needed me; this was a magnificent man, one worthy of my time and energy.

Because Edna was family, I had known John a long time. He and Edna taught my sister and me how to play bridge when we were youngsters. When I was fourteen I spent a few weeks with them in their home in Moore's Mills, N.Y. John was a handsome man then in his late thirties, a hard-working provider for Edna and their two young children, Michael and Cathy. He was also compassionate. When Edna's young nephew found a date for me with a teen I didn't respect or enjoy, John lifted my dour mood by taking me to a movie and buying me an ice cream soda after. His was an innocent gesture but, for a young impressionable girl, a huge lesson in how a gentleman treats a lady. Of course, Edna sent me home after that. She could see I was developing a crush on her husband.

Years later there were good times, mostly with Edna, as John would often be working in another state or another country when either I'd visit or Edna would visit me. John was the chief financial officer of a nascent computer company at a time when computer technology had to be vigorously sold to companies ignorant of the potential of cyberspace. It was also a time when CFOs did double and triple duty as sales representatives and chief problem solvers. John traveled to places where his skills were needed. Edna and I were very close. I could feel her love for me in her interest in my welfare; she often had good advice. I cherished her as a second mother. John seemed more private to me, perhaps because he always appeared to defer to Edna in public. It was she who made all the social decisions and he, who as a gracious host, focused on the needs and comfort of the guests they had.

When in 1984 I began my studies at Saybrook University, an external degree graduate school in San Francisco, I stayed with Edna and John whenever the school required my presence for residential learning. Frankly, John was an appendage to the relationship Edna and I had. He drove the car to the places Edna wanted me to see and paid the bills when we ate at restaurants she wanted us to sample. He was cheerful, but not as much involved with me as Edna was.

On one of my visits John was suffering pains from kidney stones and was being ignored. Since he had a habit of complaining and worrying about dire circumstances every time something minor happened to him, these exaggerated protests became so familiar that the family dismissed them as hypochondria. Edna got used to ignoring them. A major health problem, however, brought out the stoic in John; he'd suffer silently.

On this occasion the kidney stone pains were so bad that John mentioned his discomfort. I was sympathetic. Edna, however, was dressed and ready for a car ride to Stanford University where I could purchase textbooks I needed. "Don't worry about him," she said to me. "He's okay." I wanted to take care of John, but my needs, in Edna's eyes, took priority: a hurting John drove us to the bookstore.

When we got back to their apartment, John stretched out on the living room rug in an effort to relieve his pain. Because of his sacrifice for me, I decided to do something for him. I knelt down beside him and massaged his back. Unknowingly, I was planting seeds that would begin to grow when a grieving John came to Hawaii.

John had many more kidney stone attacks until he was forced by fate to take action after Edna had a serious operation in July 1985. In a cruel irony, Edna had developed kidney cancer. Since her illness was diagnosed during my trip to San Francisco for a school residential requirement in June of that year, I became a natural part of her support system. In September, John, recognizing Edna's need for his strength, decided to address his own health problem. His kidney stones were removed by lithotripsy. After the procedure, he gave up his hobbies and business interests and devoted himself full-time to caring for Edna until she died in July of 1986.

It seems especially hard for a man to lose his mate. Living alone was agony to John. He could get through the day with its chores and personal care business, but twilight brought on deep melancholy and depression. Nights were sleepless exercises mingled with a hope, never realized, that he'd dream of Edna. His visits with friends became an imposition on them for he couldn't stop talking about his misery.

If he wasn't talking, he was brooding. Family could help only so much as family members were busy living their own lives, moving on. John was stuck. Moreover, he was resentful that others couldn't appreciate the pain he was feeling and wouldn't take the time to help him assuage the pain. Holding on to the pain seemed to be the only life he had now, though something deep within was moving him towards a new life.

Suffering is an abiding condition of old age. With every new year of life, aches and pains of the body surface. Teeth wear out, eyes grow dim, and ears deafen. Hearing aids amplify noise and speech sounds electronic. Having a companion to complain to, even if the companion won't listen to complaints, is essential. Even a non-responsive partner provides the opportunity for a satisfying sulk. To be alone with one's own aches and pains exaggerates them and such physical ailments mean trips to the doctor where, when nothing is found to be physically wrong, non-action often brings on frustration in a man—for a man likes results when a problem is to be solved—and shame in a woman, who can't shake the idea of intruding needlessly on someone else's important time.

John made many trips to Hawaii and I to San Francisco after his initial trip. In January 1987 on my first trip to the Menlo Park apartment where now only John lived he made his first physical move on me. We were in the hot tub of the pool area of the apartment complex. No one else was there. Flushed by the exercise of an early morning swim and the soothing heat of the Jacuzzi, we sat together and talked. Words, too, were soothing. Suddenly, John reached for me, pulling on the strap of my bathing suit, his hand on my bare breast.

"No, John, no," I said gently and put up my hand to push him away, hoping not to embarrass him by my rejection for I was very fond of him, very sympathetic to his plight.

He pulled away abruptly. "Let's go inside," he said.

We did. I made us breakfast and we spent the day reading the paper and doing odd chores around the house. He took me out to supper where he apologized.

"I'm sorry. I'm really sorry," he said. He was contrite, tearful, ashamed and full of guilt, both because of my marital status and because he felt unfaithful to Edna. Even in death, the bond between husband and wife is so strong (especially after a good marriage) that any movement towards a new relationship can seem like infidelity.

"It's okay, John," I assured him. "I understand. You are grieving. Don't be so hard on yourself." I really believed the situation was under control.

However, the need for someone to be there to share intimacy with him was stronger than John's shame in being unfaithful to Edna; he came back for more that night, entering the bedroom where I was sleeping, waking me with the weight of his body on mine. This time I didn't push him away. I allowed the intimacy. It seemed cruel to deny comfort to someone I loved. Even though inwardly I disavowed that love, the love I truly felt for John would not allow me to deny him comfort.

Afterwards, I had guilt feelings of my own to deal with. The act of being unfaithful, no matter how justified, was too much for me to bear alone. When I got home, I told

Ted what had happened. He was very angry, very hurt. Oddly, I cared, but I didn't really care. Ted's reaction was understandably centered on his own feelings of betrayal. However, I sensed that his security was even more threatened, so I used learned skills to soothe my husband's hurt and persuade him that John not only needed me, but that, in his grief, John needed us both.

Ted liked John. John was a kindly father figure to him who paid attention to Ted's stories about his work and suggested ways of improving his position with his bosses and co-workers. Ted, in turn, was sympathetic to John's grief and open to making him comfortable in our home until John became physical with me. When I explained to Ted that it must certainly have been grief and opportunity that caused the trespass, coupled with my own long history of love for John and Edna, he calmed. My arguments must have seemed reasonable, for Ted agreed to have John come to stay with us again. I left the impression with my husband that another incident would not occur—truly thinking I was being honest. Eventually, John decided to make Hawaii his home.

So began a period when the three of us lived together in Hawaii. John had his own room; my husband and I had ours.

Ted began to spend long periods at night away from the house, which was fine with me. John and I spent time together during the day, going to the beach, and at night just being together, talking not only of his grief but also of my dreams and ambitions. He supported my pursuit of my doctorate and gave me advice on the business aspects of my psychotherapy practice. Our views of the world were similar and informed as were our interests in music and theater. Even in his grief, John was richly attuned to life, a contrast to my low-keyed husband. John and I looked for apartments, yet he never found a place that suited him, for none came with a built-in companion. During the early months of this arrangement, John and I were chaste. Perhaps our being in the home with Ted there made the difference. Perhaps the sheer comfort of having a home with people in it who loved him was enough for John.

One night Ted was sharp with me, making a remark that stung. It must have been obvious to him that I was letting go of the thin connection we now had. He had been moody, going out alone at night without any disapproval from me; I was content with John's company. I don't remember what Ted said; I remember only the impact for Ted was not ordinarily given to sharp remarks. Ignoring my sudden tear-filled eyes, he turned and walked out of the house. John, his eyes soft with sympathy for me, put his arms around me and gave me a soft, healing kiss. Not long after that I told my husband our marriage was over. John returned to his daughter's home in California, leaving Ted and me to work out the details of our divorce.

Chapter Five:
Chinese Daughters
(2008)

John and I were together for 20 years, or were we? Do we count as the very beginning—that "so beautiful" in the Honolulu Airport four months after Edna died? Or was the beginning when the first physical desire surfaced in San Francisco two months later? Or, maybe it all began when John finally left California to come to live with me in Hawaii, almost two years to the day that Edna died.

I used to tease him that he was allowed only 16 years with me, since I divorced two husbands, after relationships that, coincidentally, ended after 16 years with each one. He'd tease back, always pushing forward in years the date we became a couple, so that we'd never reach the 16-year mark. Our teasing created such confusion that we lost track of anniversaries, neither of us really willing to contemplate separation.

In our time together, we moved from Hawaii to California to be closer to John's children. We learned to live in our community of active older adults, spending time swimming in one of the pools or attending club meetings. We were politically active, particularly in organizations that sought civil rights for the oppressed. I wrote a column for lesbian and gay publications as I had in Hawaii and both John and I wrote and published books. We attended events at the graduate school where I had finished my degree. We also traveled, visiting friends and family and made a couple of trips to Europe. We had relationship problems that we tackled and resolved and we had fun together.

Together. The word brings melancholy to me. The time of togetherness is gone now, alive only in memory. What does it matter anymore how long we were together? The years allotted to a happy relationship are never enough.

When I feel sorry for myself, sorry that the years have irretrievably vanished, there is no room for gratitude for what I had been given in those years. People who remark that I will always have my fond memories for comfort are likely to see a brief antipathetic frown as response. What good are fond memories? Who makes meaning of memories when life's meaning is gone? In the early months of grief I often felt crazy, as if life was going on around me while I simply existed, breathing without taking in any sustenance for my spirit, a spirit on hiatus.

With John gone, I found myself envious of the relationships my friends still had with husbands and impatient with people who didn't appreciate their relationships. On a bus trip to a casino, led by seniors in my community, I was seated alone in front of a couple that was bickering. She was mercilessly faulting him for everything that had gone wrong that morning, last week, last year and the whole of their lives. "We wouldn't have been late, George, if you had gotten up in time. I don't know why you always embarrass me like this. You'd sleep your life away if I hadn't married you. Lots of good that did me."

He was snapping back with a criticism of her never-ending complaints about him. "Oh for God's sake let go of it, will you? You aren't happy unless you have something to complain about."

"Not true, George. If you would just set your alarm and then get up when it rings. I've told you this a hundred times."

It wasn't even the words they were using that bothered me. It was their tone. I wanted to turn around and shake them. I wanted to shout at them to stop the harangue between them and look for the love that had brought them together in the first place. Moreover, I wanted to cry because I had no one to chastise or cherish me. I sat tearless, staring ahead, wishing the trip over.

Fighting an impulse to be gloomy was difficult in the first months after John's death. I wasn't enthusiastic about attending the Lifetime Learning course in which I'd enrolled. I struggled with trying not to resent the need to participate at a meaningful level in a fund-raising campaign to build a new pre-school building at the church I had chosen. Finding someone to use John's subscription theater and symphony tickets brought the necessity of being festive with that someone until the lights dimmed and no one could see the tears in my eyes or hear the stifled sobs.

Looking back, I'm grateful for the people who were patient with me. My friends kept me going by going places with me, by letting me talk when I needed to talk and hugging me when I needed hugging. Human touch is so important. Without it, most of us would starve emotionally. We need to know we matter at any age. Such affirmations come in words, but are most sincerely felt when accompanied by touch, a hand on the shoulder, a kiss on the check, or a big bear hug of appreciation.

In June of that first year of mourning, I wandered into the Farmer's Market in our retirement community and idly stopped by a table with information on a program of cultural home stay for foreign students. The director of the program asked if I would host in my home a student from China for three weeks beginning in July. I raised some objections, but she assured me all my objections would be met with reasonable solutions and so, impulsively, I agreed.

Soon I had a visit from the director and an assistant, armed with letters and pictures from two very charming 13-year-old Chinese girls who asked me if they could be my "Chinese daughters." How could I resist? Lily and Juliet came to me on a warm July evening, fatigued by their long plane trip and transport from the San Francisco Airport, but awake enough to remember their manners, digging in their suitcases for small gifts of appreciation for their American mother before plopping their weary bodies into the bed I'd made for them.

The two girls were friends in their hometown of Chongqing. I had been a 7th and 8th grade teacher in Hawaii, a multicultural state with many Asian-American residents. From the beginning Lily and Juliet (their chosen American names) seemed very familiar to me in looks and actions. We bonded quickly for I knew a little bit about the psychology of thirteen-year-olds and their Chinese culture wasn't totally new to me.

Feeding them in the morning, seeing that they had lunch with them or plans for lunch before they left for school, taking them to the bus stop or picking them up in the afternoon gave me a sense of being useful once more. Their youthful energy, their need for advice from me, and especially their calls of "Mom!" when they wanted something, filled me with joy. I found myself happy, really happy again.

What a contrast to taking care of John. Now I was involved in young lives, lives that were enthusiastic and healthy, looking for experience in a new country. I worked closely with Lily and Juliet and their teachers. I went on field trips with them being careful not to require them to sit with me at lunch, since like most teens they wanted to sit with their friends. I was there to hold their purses or their packages and to answer questions, but never to intrude. At home I allowed them to converse with one another in Chinese with the condition that I could ask them about their conversation if I wanted to and I did ask frequently. They began to interrupt their chatter to tell me in English what had happened at school and what was going on with their friends, including me in their interests, as they would have their own mothers.

They made me a Chinese meal, using my pots and my stove. I taught them how to fry eggs, laughing together at Lily's puzzlement over cracking an egg. They didn't cook at home, so I was especially proud of their efforts to make a wonderful meal and their sensitivity to my tastes in not putting chili peppers in my portion. I tried to make American meals that would appeal to them, but usually they'd say they preferred their own "hot pot" entrees. They did like pizza, however, and MacDonald's hamburgers and fries. I took them to a Chinese restaurant, which they found totally inadequate and found the American-style Chinese our server spoke to them inadequate as well.

I introduced them to my church. Coming from a secular China, they were wary, but polite, and decided after a first visit that they didn't want to go to church again. Unwilling to leave them home alone, I insisted that they come with me, but allowed them to stay outside in the picnic area and play card games. At the end of the worship hour, they drank hot chocolate and socialized with the congregants. By the end of their visit, to my immense pleasure, they asked to attend the worship service once more. This gesture was an exquisite act of manners and respect for me and respect for the churchgoers they had grown to like.

We developed an easy flow of life together. On weekends I took them to movies that they might enjoy, especially the Disney film *Wall-E* and *Up the Yangtze,* a documentary set in their home territory in China. The Disney film, short on dialogue and long in action, was easily understood and *Up the Yangtze* gave them satisfaction in hearing their home language and challenge in deciphering the English in the film. One weekend, we went to the county fair where they were impressed with the flower show and loved the carnival rides. I had brought two younger women friends with me who were able to keep up with the boundless energy of the girls and go on rides with them. On another weekend, Lily and Juliet played in a local park with visiting grandchildren of another friend of mine. Suddenly, my life made sense again.

Always there seemed to be new gifts coming from their suitcases, small representations of China—tea from the fields of Chongqing, a fan, a stone with a carved Buddha face, a red Chinese good luck ribbon which I hung on a light fixture in the hall. One gift, a round clear plastic Buddha, they placed reverently next to John's funeral card on the mantel and, with their hands folded, bowed in respect to my late partner. I was deeply touched.

Lily and Juliet were with me for three weeks, including four weekends. I was conscious and grateful for the blessing of their presence, but not yet aware enough to acknowledge any spiritual growth. When they left, I sensed I had changed for the better. Still, I was not done with grief. It was only seven months since John had died, and, with the girls gone, I began to feel at loose ends once more.

A pervasive sadness appeared yet again, a sadness fed by Dom's serious illness and Pat's progressive dementia. Dom and Pat were good friends of ours. John and I met them in 1993 when we joined the New Yorkers, a social club that Pat started. Through the years we shared joyful times in our retirement community. We'd go to dinner dances together, Pat and Dom doing their long- practiced routine of the Peabody, a dance similar to the Jitterbug of my era. (Pat and Dom were closer to John's age than mine.) There were club meetings, parties and picnics and outings to San Francisco. We even went to Hawaii together twice, one trip to celebrate with me a book reading I was doing at Barnes and Noble.

When Dom began to need oxygen for his lung disease and Pat's dementia made her speech increasingly incoherent, John and I would visit giving as much cheer as we could and sharing their pleasure in our being there. John scolded Dom if he mentioned consequences to his poor health saying he expected Dom to be at *his* funeral, not to go to Dom's. John died on December 17, 2007. That week, I brought the obituary in the local paper to Dom and Pat. She was sleeping and Dom, in his pajamas and blue robe with the oxygen tubes trailing from his nose, met me in the middle of the room, his arms stretched to enfold me. We wailed, long and loud, alternately flailing our arms and holding on to one another in a deeply felt sadness, bereaved at the loss of John, bereaved by the loss of the person we had known as Pat and bereaved at what was to come for Dom.

When one grows old, there seems to be no end to losses. It's as if life takes from us more than it gives, perhaps in a preview of our own eventual withdrawal, our own demise. We reconcile ourselves to the experience of loss. We laugh at losing our figures or expanding our waistline. We accept thinning hair and drying skin, although we keep the cosmetic business prosperous in trying to recapture some of our youthful good looks. We keep on living in the face of these kinds of losses, but how do you reconcile yourself to the loss of a friend? Friendship with its treasure of memories, with all the common joys and camaraderie and even the problems tackled and resolved in the name of shared values, does not easily yield nor can it easily be replaced. It's as if a part of own existence leaves when a friend leaves us.

I began to visit Dom and Pat, periodically, throughout 2008, sharing with them pictures of my Chinese daughters that July and, eventually, my plans to take a Mediterranean cruise in the fall and to spend a couple of days in Venice. Being Italian, both were interested in the trip, although Pat only told me so with the brightness in her eyes. I was worried about leaving when Dom was so ill, but he encouraged me to go, assuaging my fears with the promise that he'd still be among the living when I returned.

John had promised me a trip to Venice. I wanted to go to complete that promise. Others who have lost spouses talk about the urge to travel. Maybe physically moving away from grieving and into new places has the allure of providing renewal to life. I hoped for such a transformation.

None of my friends wanted to spend the money to go with me. The trip was expensive; I wavered in my decision to go. When a chance storm tore the heart out of my beloved ash tree in front of the house and the homeowners' association decided its remains had to be cut down, I cried inconsolably. First John, and now, my tree. Enough! I called the travel agency that day and committed myself to the trip.

Chapter Six:
More Grief
(2008–2009)

I am a member of a women's group that meets every Wednesday morning for two and a half hours. We have been together since 1996, and though our membership has varied through the years, a core group of five has remained.

We are more than friends to one another. We are healers. Listening to the concerns we have for ourselves, our families and friends, we speak to one another in soft tones of empathy or gently nudge one another out of negativity by giving fresh perspective on perplexing problems, or we laugh with each other over the absurdities in our lives. We've shepherded one another through minor irritations we've had with husbands and partners to major health problems in ourselves and in our loved ones. We've grieved our losses together, but we've never allowed any of us to get lost in grief. We've celebrated birthdays and anniversaries, have gone to museums and exhibits together and have studied and discussed alternative healings, once attending a psychological conference together.

As we've aged, we've had to face breakdowns in our bodies, pain that for some of us is unrelenting, and the loss of cherished relationships either to serious illness or to death. Still, we meet every Wednesday and the talk is unfailingly optimistic. Anne, our oldest member is our role model. Despite her constant pain, she keeps moving, does daily exercise, goes places with her family and friends, and keeps reading and going to lectures and classes. She may wear out in time, but she certainly won't rust out. We younger ones get the message: If Anne can do it, so can we!

When I told my group that I was considering the Mediterranean cruise, they enthusiastically urged me to go. I was concerned about the cost of the trip; my income dropped when John died. My friends assured me that I could afford to go and that I should go. A major attraction of the cruise was a seminar on classical music with a well-known musicologist as a lecturer and a classical pianist aboard to provide concerts. John had loved classical music, and so I had grown to love it, too, watching him listen with such pleasurable intensity that any pain or worry he had would vanish from his features. I hoped not only to learn more about classical music, but also to experience it deeply in a fantasy trip aboard a ship in the blue Mediterranean Sea.

Still, planning a trip without John was painful. I'd be alone. I'd be uncoupled, a single, walking the deep carpeted planks of the ship without the support of a mate. How to act? How to engage with others, especially in a ship full of couples? How to make decisions on food and tours?

My friends calmed my fears. Go, they urged. Go.

The night before I flew out to board the ship in Barcelona, Steve came to stay with me. He drove two and a half hours from his home in San Jose so he could take me to the San Francisco airport. I could have taken a bus or driven my own car to one of those hotels with long-term parking accommodations; I was accustomed to being independent.

However, Steve, always a good son, became more sensitive to my needs, after John died, and stepped in to provide the sense of security John had given me on drives to the airport.

On the plane I fought to control the grief that threatened to well up inside me. I felt so alone, flying thousands of miles from home without a partner to share the pains and pleasure of travel. Whatever was to be on this trip was mine to create. Could I, would I find the joy I sought? *Stop it*, I told myself. *Grieve when you get home.* What is the use of spending so much time, energy and resources on a trip if I'm going to use it for grieving?

My admonition to myself didn't work and, as the jet engines droned, I kept thinking about John and the last few years of his life. That slow, steady decline that robbed him of his dignity, the embarrassing loss of control, not only of basic bodily functions, but also of his balance, and, eventually, the necessity to accept his total reliance on me. The sadness that filled his eyes as he struggled to find a way back to his old self broke my heart. He had tried so hard to stand on his own two feet, to keep his dignity even as he fell eighteen times in the last months of his life. He didn't want me to call 911 and I didn't want to call, and yet, I was so exhausted, suffering pains and injury myself from trying to help him get up; I had to call for help. Ultimately, I had to put him in a care facility. This thinking triggered further grief. I shuddered.

My seatmate, absorbed in a book he was reading, was totally unaware of my situation. Not wanting to come unglued and place my burdens inappropriately on him, I began looking for positives to replace the grief. I closed my eyes and remembered how supportive our families had been to us.

Cathy, John's daughter, and Charmaine, his son's wife had come several times to tend to him while I took breaks from the care giving. They willingly took on roles as chefs, housekeepers and nurses for John and gave me time to travel for much needed rest and a change of scenery. Middle-aged women with families of their own, Cathy and Charmaine became like sisters under one roof, exchanging views on life, sharing tips on cooking and jewelry making, and laughing over silly antics of children and grandchildren. Their presence brought a fresh breeze of restored interest in life to John as he happily listened to them and was tenderly cared for and listened to by them. His son Michael called and visited frequently. John was so proud of his college professor son and the recognition he had won in his work. John, himself, was unable to go to college because he graduated from high school in 1929, the year of the Great Depression stock market crash. He was lucky enough to find a job and help his father support the family. With Michael, John could talk business and the state of the economy of the world, adding anecdotes from his own experience and listening carefully to his son's analyses.

Rita, John's sister, called every week and still calls me. In December 2006, Rita's son, named John after his uncle, arranged a surprise for John's 95th birthday in flying Rita and his wife Ann from New York to California.

As Cathy and her husband Randy and I awaited their arrival, we had to make up stories on why the birthday dinner wasn't ready yet, for our visitors were delayed in coming from the airport. "Oh, guess what!" I told John. "I forgot to put the potatoes on. It will be at least another half hour before we eat." He nodded, unaware of our conspiracy.

When the doorbell rang, and Rita walked into our living room, John looked in her direction and, for a moment, didn't know who she was. "Rita," he finally said, astonished at her appearance. "What are you doing here?"

"What?" Rita exclaimed. "You don't know your own sister?" They laughed then. John rose, unassisted, from his chair. The sheer adrenalin of happy surprise propelled him upward. Rita went to him and we onlookers smiled at the sight of brother and sister embracing in a joyful reunion.

As the plane hit an air pocket, I laughed out loud, rejoicing in the happy memory of John and Rita. My seatmate looked up from his book, but didn't say anything. I smiled, weakly, and went back to my reverie.

I thought about how responsive Steve and the rest of the family were to my needs. Steve sat vigil with me in the hospital before my breast reduction surgery in July 2006, while John, physically unable to accompany me, stayed home by himself for the few hours Steve was gone. After the operation and while I was in the hospital, Steve stayed with John until Cathy arrived. She was to take care of John and me the first week I was home; the following week it was Steve's partner Dave who cared for us. In May 2007, Steve came alone to help put John, temporarily, in a care home and be with me, again, during and after my gall bladder surgery. How fortunate I have been to have a family so willing to help.

I sighed contentedly. The positive memories had calmed me; I gave in to the monotony of marking travel time with the drink-meal-movie-snacks-and-music rituals of crossing the Atlantic. My seat partner, snoring now with his book resting on his chest, dreamed of his own issues, thankfully oblivious to mine.

Eventually, I arrived in Barcelona. My suitcase didn't. My lips trembled when I reported the loss to baggage handlers. I hate publicly appearing weak and vulnerable, but I was exhausted by jet lag and the long, tedious hours of travel. The prospect of cruising without a change of clothes set me on the verge of tears. A stream of travelers left the area while I conducted the unpleasant business. When I was done, there was no one left in the area but me and a forlorn, empty baggage carrousel. Some welcome to Spain!

I stumbled through the heavy security doors and into the outer public area, certain no one waited for me. I was wrong. The ship had sent greeters. They scooped me up, took me to a waiting van, assured me they would take care of my lost luggage, and bid me sit back and relax.

My good humor returned when, aboard the huge cruise liner, I "shopped" in the ship's closet of multiple items of clothing left behind by former passengers. The selection was awful, but I had been in my traveling clothes a long, long time. So, after a shower and a nap, wearing the comforting terrycloth robe the cruise line provided, I got dressed. I put on a ballooning rust-colored slipover blouse and the dark slacks I'd been wearing. I took the belt from the terrycloth robe and used it to corral the blouse into a waistline. I decorated myself with a green stone necklace Dave had made for me, and as an added fillip, put on the thin beige socks the airline had given us passengers as comforters for sore travel feet. I felt like an international fashion designer.

Off I went to explore the ship, its amazing spa facilities, pools, restaurants, library, meeting rooms, casino, and bar areas. In one of these areas a band was playing. I sat down to drink a glass of cranberry juice and listen to old 1940's tunes, heartbreakers born out of the loneliness of the war years. I was tearing up once more, and again, I scolded myself. *Is this trip about fun or grieving for John?* I got up, marched directly to the bandleader and told him my husband had died; would he please play some upbeat tunes? He apologized and immediately switched his band to playing snappy bossa nova and sweet jazz.

I tapped my foot and then noticed couples entering the area. Another challenge. How to bridge the gap between single and coupled? I got up and approached some friendly-looking faces. "My luggage got lost," I began, "but look at the snazzy casual outfit I made from the ship's closet!" I pirouetted in a model's style, and they laughed with me. Encouraged, I vowed I'd make a toga out of my terry cloth robe for the next night's formal dinner, if my luggage didn't arrive. They laughed again. I began to feel as if I fit in, after all, even though my status was still so unfamiliar to me.

At dinner, I met people from Northern California, close enough to where I lived that I felt I knew them. They were part of the group that had signed up for the classical music seminar. I also found out that, since the person who was to be my assigned roommate brought along a friend to room with, I'd have my cabin to myself, a fortunate happening, for I did not have to adjust to a stranger in my room. Sufficient were the life adjustments I was making to the stranger in me.

I went to bed that night, thinking I had done well. I'd overcome the day's hardships without giving into helplessness and despair. I had asserted myself and acted positively to ward off grief and bring into consciousness an anticipation of good times. I had found and used my humor to connect with others.

My luggage arrived the night before we sailed from Barcelona. We were in port for only one day, a day I spent on the ship since I had seen Barcelona on an earlier trip and was too tired, physically and emotionally to attempt a tour.

Before I left on my trip my sister Marion, living in Delaware, fell and broke her hip. Marion is ten years older than I; the concern was whether she'd survive the ordeal of an operation and rehabilitation. She still wasn't fully recovered from a stroke four years earlier. My younger sister, Flo, had doubts. I felt guilty knowing I was going on a pleasure trip while my sisters were struggling with these issues. Marion, like Dom, assured me that she would be all right and that I should go. Flo gave me no such assurance and stopped speaking to me altogether. There are deeper issues between Flo and me that culminated in this reaction. Our sibling rivalries, never fully resolved, trigger both vocal and implied criticism of one another. A recess in our relationship proves beneficial to us both, even though such a break has a grief of its own.

During the trip, I kept thinking about Marion and wrote her two long letters to let her know she was in my thoughts. In Rome, when I went to the public audience with the Pope, I felt that the pontiff blessed her when he prayed for those who were suffering and ill. I deeply felt how tenuous life is and contemplated the loss of this sister when I dared. I knew I'd need to prepare for this eventuality, but did the preparation have to come when I was trying to heal my grief over John?

As the trip progressed I found two younger women who had lost mates and we consoled one another to a point. The women were friends and were also trying to find joy in the trip, as was I. After a time, they moved away from me. I understood; grief can be overwhelming and confession of one's deepest feelings brings on even deeper feelings and fear of vulnerability.

The onboard classes in the classical music seminar were wonderful. Our musicologist James Keller was knowledgeable and tailored his lessons to the trip itself. We took a virtual cruise with well-known composers as they touched ports in the Mediterranean that had inspired their lives and their music. Yet it was the music itself that flowed and danced its way into my heart giving me comfort and a sense of eternal life. How long this music itself has lived! How long it shall live after I have gone!

When Awadagin Pratt, our classical pianist, gave his concerts, he insisted all thirteen class participants sit on the stage with him, a move that entwined our beings with his talent. His recital of *Brahms Variation and Fugue On a Theme by Handel, Opus 24* and the *Bach/Pratt Passacaglia and Fugue in C Minor* were brilliant. The music soared and so did my mood. In another concert Awadagin played an open, huge and very emotional *Sonata in B Minor* by Franz Liszt. This time my tears were stirred, not by grief, but by the music, its performance and by the tears in Awadagin's own eyes.

I made casual friends among the passengers and, in particular, a couple from New Jersey who kept a protective eye on me whenever we got off the ship together. The ship tours of the countries we visited were both exhilarating and exhausting. I felt at times bounced from steep hills of Monaco to the Leaning Tower of Pisa and to the Trevi Fountain in Rome before moving into a Greek myth at Epidaurus. At the Epidaurus amphitheater one can speak in a whisper and be heard throughout the theater. Most visitors say something for the thrill of it. I stood stage center and began to sing "Side by Side." Soon, my shipmates gathered round and sang with me. No Maria Callas, I, though she stood in the same spot as I was standing, yet the music and the camaraderie filled me with happiness.

There were quiet times on the ship when I stood at the rail and thought of John. I wouldn't allow the tears that wanted release and silently apologized to him for holding back my feelings. I felt John would understand. He had told me when he was alive not to grieve for him, as if that were possible.

In Corfu, Greece, a strange and haunting thing happened. I sat in the square in Old Town in front of an ancient Catholic church where a woman with the voice of an angel was singing in English. Enchanted, I went into the church and sat in a pew as she sang of her desire to give me Jesus for "then I have given you everything." After finishing her song, she left without a word, just disappeared. I didn't see her go. I was mystified, but I knew I had experienced a moment of deep spiritual significance for my grieving heart grew quiet there.

From Greece we sailed into beautiful Croatia and toured its ancient walled city and then sailed for Venice. This is the city I most wanted to see, the promised mecca from

John. As we glided into Venice, a guide, through the ship's intercom, pointed out places of interest that rose out of the foggy morning mist. One wonderful scene after another unfolded in a rapid eye-filling feast. It was all too much for me. I hurried back to my cabin where I finally let John in. I talked to him. I told him how much I missed him, how I wished he could be here in Venice with me, and how I wished I could please feel his spirit with me. There was just the dark stillness of the cabin. No Venice. No John. I let tears flow freely. At last, I gave sorrow its due.

Chapter Seven:
As If I Were Whole Again
(2008-2009)

I sat on a red velvet seat in the middle of the gondola, not alone, but alone in my thoughts. My fantasies of being in Venice were coming true. I was with a gondolier who was singing as he paddled into a peaceful canal. Buildings framed our passage under picturesque bridges from which good-natured people waved. I thought of John. Yes, it would have been nice for him to be sitting here with me, but I didn't dwell on that thought. I noted that, for once, I didn't feel grief. I was too happy, too caught up in the romantic revelry we gondola mates felt on a moonlit night in Venice. So what if the ride was outrageously expensive! So what if we were in an armada of twenty or so gondolas in an obviously commercial tourist event! So what if a recorded *O Sole Mio* drifted toward us from a designated music gondola. We simply encouraged our gondolier to sing in his own voice and, when he did, we sang with him. Happy, happy music. I felt a quiet satisfaction.

That morning I had toured the Doges Palace. Our Venetian guide was angry. He showed us painting after beautiful painting, which he maligned. "Copies," he spat out. The city fathers had capitulated to Napoleon over 200 years ago, surrendering the city to France; most of the treasured paintings in the Doges Palace were violated—stripped from the walls and sent to France to be paraded in public as spoils of the winner. "Inferior," he snapped as he showed us the difference in the coloring of a copied painting compared to one that had somehow survived. I loved the passion of the moment. I loved that someone cared about what happened to good art and, even after the interval of two centuries, could still bristle at such unforgivable governmental betrayal! The guide's Italian indignation reminded me of John's wont to be equally and vocally contemptuous of injustice. He would have been at home here.

I was still in a good mood late that night as I boarded the ship for the last time. We were housed in port as a convenience to us in touring Venice, and now it was time to go back to my cabin, pack and get ready to disembark in the morning. I was confident I could find my way to my hotel the next day because there was a landing stage for the waterbuses right at the pier where our liner was docked. All I had to do was get on the bus, get off at the proper stop and go to my hotel.

What a rude awakening the next day when I got off the ship to find the landing stage area closed. Apparently, this area is used only when liners are disembarking tourists who go into town and spend their money, not for those going home as most of the passengers were. I was told that a land bus would take me to a plaza where I could get a waterbus to St. Mark's Square where my hotel was located. Alas, the buses refused to take me. They were headed to the airport. My only options were to walk, not knowing where I was going, or to take a land taxi.

I opted for the taxi even though it cost 30 euro, which I knew was too expensive. Instead of immediately taking me to my destination, the driver hustled two other women into taking the ride with us and charged them 25 euro for both of them! Suddenly, Venice wasn't romantic anymore. Outraged, I protested loudly, "No! You won't treat me differently." John would have been proud. I browbeat the driver into giving me a discount as well. "Okay, lady. Okay. I give you discount. Wait."

When we got to the plaza, he handed me five euro and turned to leave. I felt like spitting out an epithet in the style of the Doges Palace guide—if only I knew a curse in Italian—but I was tired and out of ammunition. I took my bags and tried to stomp away, only the little bag kept falling off the bigger one, which was on rollers. You can't stomp with a bag on rollers.

I was wary when I bought a two-day pass at the transportation terminal, but the transaction here was official and straightforward. I followed others as they boarded the waterbus for St. Mark's Square and sat with my bags at my feet, watching the city reveal itself. It seemed strange to travel along the edge of the city in a boat and see people walking or tending to their daily business as we passed. There are many islands that make up the city of Venice, islands connected by bridges. Most of the islands do not have cars. The people walk or take waterbuses from one point to another just as I was doing. When I got off the waterbus, I would be walking to my hotel.

I began to get nervous. What was I doing here? I was on my own. It was early in the morning; I wouldn't be welcome at the hotel until later in the afternoon. Would I even find the hotel? I wanted to grab someone and ask if he or she would be my pal, but the bus was full of locals weary with their workday underway and probably weary of lost and loony tourists. Some of my friends certainly thought me loony to be on my own in a foreign country without the backup of a companion to fight my traveler's anxieties.

Long ago I had learned to fend for myself. In the early 60's I was a young Navy wife traveling to Japan with two toddler sons. Arriving at night in the country without hotel reservations was a loony thing to do. My Naval aviator husband was flying intelligence runs over Viet Nam from a carrier out at sea and certainly was out of contact with me. Through a helpful taxi driver and some other Navy wives following their husbands, we landed safely in a bachelor officer quarters' room for the night. Later, I found a house for us on the local economy without speaking a word of Japanese! I was used to being independent and solving problems. Of course, I get butterflies in my stomach in a new situation, but I never feel helpless.

At the edge of St. Mark's Square I began to laugh at myself and relax. The worst thing that could happen would be that I'd get lost. How lost can you get in St. Mark's Square? It's huge, yet compact, and full of landmarks as reliable as a compass.

Of course, I found my hotel, left my bags with the concierge and went out to look for lunch. I found a charming outdoor restaurant near the gondola station of the evening before, and I ate a genuine Italian pizza and drank nearly a quart of water as the work of the day had dehydrated me. The sun was warm, the day pleasant and the breezes of Venice caressed me.

After lunch, I still didn't know what to do with myself. I couldn't sit in St. Mark's Square because there were no freestanding benches or chairs. Every seat was attached to an establishment that required something be purchased for the privilege of sitting. I went into the Basilica of San Marco instead, paying not only to see the magnificent home of the bones of St. Mark, but also to sit in the benches in the chapel on the side. A sign in English stated that the pews were reserved for those who wished to pray. I wished to rest, so, I sat in those holy pews in what I hoped looked like an attitude of prayer, casting an eye to the side, now and then, to check on whether chapel police were checking on me.

My energy restored, I went outside and took pictures. When I grew weary of that and walking through the ever-present pigeons that define and occasionally defile St. Mark's Square, I paid some more euros to take the elevator to the top of the bell tower and take still more pictures.

So this is what it is really like, traveling on one's own in one of the most romantic settings in the world! I thought I'd be sad, but I wasn't sad. I felt strangely empowered, satisfied with what I had done. I began to love where I was. Even if I was by myself, *I was by myself in Venice!* To paraphrase Frost's famous poem, 'twas the road less traveled' that made all the difference.

My hotel room was tiny with no view from a shuttered window over the alley that served as a Venetian street. Still it was clean. The shower was so small, I feared my body would get stuck in the stall, but I managed. I slept a few hours and then went out for the night life—a good dinner in a sidewalk café, strolling past shop after shop, some with intriguing Venetian masks, many with the blown glass that is world-famous, or *imitations* of the world famous glass, and then home for a night's sleep.

The next day I ate the breakfast supplied by the hotel, walked a bit and did some shopping and then decided I'd take a waterbus to Burano, an island where lace is made. I thought I'd see women busy at the task of hand-making lace. Finding the right waterbus was challenging. I got on and off several until I was assured I was on the right one. Most of the people I asked told me that I wanted to go to Murano where the serious glass blowing occurs, but no, I insisted on Burano. The waterbus plodded along, stopping at several islands in the hour's long trip. Finally, I got off on an island that was basically one street, full of colorful shops, all selling lace, mostly machine-made items. There were no women making lace—that was only for the ship passengers who had taken the paid tour the day before. I took more pictures and waited until a waterbus arrived to take me back to St. Mark's Square.

Weary, that night I sought out the restaurant where I had eaten the delicious pizza. I walked up and down along the promenade next to the canal, passing gondola stations that I didn't recognize. I made several passes. I must have walked three or four miles looking for that restaurant. Finally, I concentrated on a particular gondola station and lined it up with a bridge I recognized and said to myself, "The restaurant was here. I *know* it was here." I walked perpendicular to the canal toward the buildings. On one I noticed a locked panel and on the panel was the name of the restaurant. It was then I realized the restaurant had simply packed itself up for the day—tables, chairs, umbrellas, all whisked inside out of sight. My favorite eatery was closed. Disappointed but still hungry, I tried another restaurant nearby. Their pizza was just as delicious. Besides, they served American coffee. I was ready to go home.

The next day, I got up long before the sun and boarded a water taxi at the pier next to my hotel. This craft had a powerful engine that was muted as we glided quietly through the side canals. I had a sense of being in a modern gondola slowly curving in and out among the resident buildings of Venice and under the bridges, silent now in the early morning mist. A peaceful hypnotic trance came over me. When we emerged into the open, choppy waters of the Grand Canal, my driver revved the engine and I was flung backward in my seat, hanging on for dear life as we sped toward the airport where my plane waited to take me home. Arrivederci, Venice.

Once home, there was little time to reflect on my trip. Life had some more blows to deliver. My sister Marion was in the hospital yet again. She had crossed her legs and a screw popped loose, dislocating her new hip and requiring a second operation. In rehab yet again she caught a staph infection that was difficult to cure. By Christmas she was home, weary of hospitals and rehabs. Chastened into always using her walker, her mood and her enthusiasm for life subsided.

I was worried, aware that older people who fracture their hips often do not survive. Yet Marion had survived two hip operations and a staph infection. I wanted to hope; she is such a special sister. Her father died when she was six. By the time my father married my mother and I came along, she was ten, just the right age to become a second mother to me and, subsequently, to our younger sister Flo. Marion was a rock in our turbulent childhoods and later became fast friends with us both and our families. To have her in physical and psychological distress was disturbing. I called her, sent her pictures and a long narrative about my trip, and, in general, tried to cheer her up. There was little I could do since I lived in California and she lived in Delaware. My younger sister lived closer and talked to her daily and visited frequently. It didn't seem right, just yet, to go visit, so I kept in touch, but went on with my own life while waiting for things to get better.

Before I left on my cruise, I was asked to be on the *Together In Ministry* committee, known as TIM. Our pastor Tim Carnahan (his given name is coincidental to the committee) was in his third year of service to our church. Tim, now in his early forties, decided to become a Lutheran minister after his future wife, Debbie, took him to church. Not having grown up as a churchgoer, Tim appreciated a committee that would support him in sorting out and resolving any problems in his ministry. When first asked to be on the committee, I declined. I had joined the church by this time, but other than the monthly bridge games, I had not wanted involvement with the work of the church. My inertia was related to grieving. After a second call from a committee member, I agreed to serve.

One of my first comments to Tim was to suggest that he not wear shorts under his robe and sandals on Sunday even if the day was warm and even though Jesus wore sandals with his robes. I was on the committee to reflect the concerns of the congregants, I thought, so I did what I was supposed to do. From the look on Tim's face, I felt my foot drop, figuratively, of course, into my mouth, but he listened and began to wear slacks and dress shoes, teasing me now and then about the restrictive requirements.

I may have been getting used to the effects of my loss of John, but I still felt like a stranger in the church. There were events I could have attended—some I did, like the picnic in the fall, but mostly, I kept to myself. I didn't seem to know how to become more in the church, to feel attached to something beyond the worship I loved, the creation window, and the bridge club. I cherished two women who sat with me each Sunday, and I did join, sometimes, in the Sunday morning breakfast trips after church, but I still felt separate.

Although I had broached the subject of my grief during bridge sessions, the women listened politely, yet didn't give me much encouragement to continue revealing my feelings. After all, we were there to play cards! Besides, one of our bridge members was living with pancreatic cancer; all of us were aware of the consequences of that. It wasn't so much that I needed empathy or even sympathy. I needed to find a way to belong again, to feel secure as a person without a partner and I didn't know how to ask for that.

I often felt embarrassed by my own neediness. I should have taken care of that, I felt, when I attended a Hospice grief group three months after John died. I expected more from that group than it was able to give. Sometimes expectations get in the way of healing. The task of rebuilding my life, I was to learn, would be my own. In my seventy-third year, it didn't seem reasonable that I would have to suffer to become a person again. Didn't I do that when I was an adolescent?

One exercise I did, when asked by the Hospice grief group facilitator, was to write John a letter, which included a critique of *The Lecturer's Tale: A Novel* by James Hynes. My recollection of writing the letter was of resisting, at first, and then giving in to the feel of conversing with John. I feel a strange kind of joy, now, when I read the letter.

March 10, 2008
Dear John,

We are assigned in grief class to write a letter to our lost loved one. When I first heard of the assignment, I thought of all those letters you wrote to Edna and how I thought you were obsessive in your daily devotion to the task. I still do, I guess. I don't know how I'm coping in this healing from grief undertaking, except that I keep putting one foot in front of the other. I am tired most of the time, but I've gotten quite a bit done since you left, including your income taxes. You'll be glad to know that you owe California nothing, but the U.S. Treasury wants $633 from you. They don't care that you are dead, and that I will pay. They think, somehow, that part of the money you left for me belongs to them, and, of course, I'll pay.

This week I've enjoyed thinking about the letter. Writing it in my head was fun. Now that I'm actually doing it, it seems all the choice bits are already communicated. I finished *The Lecturer's Tale*, the book I was reading. It was a biting satire on things academic, set in a big league college, with characters more suited to a comic book than a novel. The protagonist is a sad lecturer, out of his element, and so assigned to the lowly task of teaching composition–classes held in the dingy basement of the English Department building. The more valued faculty reside eight floors up in designer-decorated offices with flunkies to cater to their every wish (yeah, I suppose college professors would love that, don't you think?) Anyway, Nelson loses a finger when he trips over something on campus just as the clock strikes thirteen on Halloween. The finger is sewed back on, but is dead, or so Nelson thinks, until it heats up on him and he discovers that he can control people, and thus, his destiny, with it. The rest of the book is a bouncy romp through Nelson's climb to the top with nutty characters saying and doing insane things. The language becomes jargonesque (see I can make up my own words, too) and I have learned a few new words and concepts from reading the book. The most interesting was the phrase *sous rapture*, which isn't in Dictionary.com, though I found an explanation for it in Wikipedia. It means, basically, that trace of image that is left after you erase something. When one character threatens Nelson with *sous rapture*, it is a delicious insult. Imagine being erased to the point where you are still seen, but are almost invisible. No, it's not kind-of-like being dead. I *knew* you'd make this about you. Yeah, yeah, the letter is about you to the extent that I am communicating with you.

I loved it the other morning when I felt you touch my left temple. It reminded me of the times you'd stop and take my head in your hands and say softly, "beautiful." I felt like you were storing up memories. Maybe now you are able to give them back with a phantom touch.

I feel comfortable with you. I thought maybe I would be frightened to think that your spirit is around, but it is quite the other way. I love it when I feel you near. You have gone before me; I feel confident that I shall see you again, and, given my age, it won't be that long either.

I know for certain how much you loved me. The daily living chores are no longer in the way; your love for me permeates my very being as much now, or, sometimes, even more than when you were alive. I know, too, how lucky we were to have one another for the time we did and to have experienced so much in life together. You were my soul mate. You gave me your best as I gave you. Thank God for that, my darling. Not all people get what we had.

I'm going to join that church I went to after you died. They are good, good people. On Easter Sunday, come and look at the flowers I ordered in your memory. They are white hyacinths. Maybe I have the wrong name for the flowers, but they are beautiful flowers given to decorate the altar in your memory and to the glory of God on Easter.

Funny, I haven't been a church member for so long. It feels good to be back. I know that going to church wasn't your thing, and so I didn't try to change you on that. I like church for the social aspect and for the quiet connection I feel with you when I am there. You used to have your Transitions group in the church, remember? I met the 96-year-old member the other day at a concert. He is still going strong and he says that the group misses you. So do I.

I'm having Jose fix all those gouges and marks in the walls and doorways that you left with your wheelchair and walker. Bless him. He is giving me a special price and tells me even if the work takes longer than he estimates, he won't charge more. It's wonderful how we were able to help his family and now he is helping me.

I love you, dear. Maybe I'll write again. Maybe I won't, but one thing I know: I will always love you and always feel near to you. Love, Kay

I talked about feeling his spirit! Where was that spirit now when December's first anniversary of John's death loomed? Did I ever really feel his spirit or was it just a stray breeze that had caressed me? Was I crazy then? Or am I going crazy now, trying to put myself back together?

No matter what I did, I thought of John. Some people in our retirement community had bought the Wii computer game console. In it is a bowling game played by swinging a remote control at a bowling alley pictured on a screen, a fun game that feels like real bowling. A bowling league was formed, and I joined. It was in those artificial bowling alleys among a group of my peers that I found myself cheering on teammates and laughing at the propensity of the ball to have a curving mind of its own when I bowled. I also sat on the sidelines and felt brooding sadness try to capture my attention; I swallowed hard to keep sobs safely unvoiced.

Our team, The Wild Turkeys, flapped our "wings" and gobbled each time one of us got a strike and did a "turkey trot" if anyone bowled three strikes in a row! Such nuttiness was a welcome relief, jarring loose sadness, reforming it into silly giggles, nuttiness at its supreme best. This kind of crazy I welcomed.

When I could no longer stand the loneliness of just me at home, I'd drive. Driving anywhere is therapy for me. During the last years of John's life, I was the one who drove the car, even the rental on our yearly trips to Hawaii. Driving without him for companionship felt strange at first, but I got used to being able to listen to the classical music station and ignore the static in the radio that would cause John to shut it off. There is a feeling of mastery, of some control of my destination that I get from driving. I feel safe behind the wheel for I was taught to drive as a youngster in a class that stressed the importance of doing things right and following the rules.

My son went on a road trip with me, as did a good friend and her son. We saw the giant coastal redwoods three hours from home. I took from the redwoods a great sense of patience, endurance, and strength. Even those that have fallen still contribute to the forest, becoming habitat for all kinds of creatures and plant life and nourishment for the soil. An old tree, still living despite being hollowed by fire, reminded me that life is too precious to give in to adversity: one can live with a deep hole in one's being.

On the anniversary of John's death I was bowling with my teammates. The day passed peacefully. That night, I lit a candle at home and thought of him; surprisingly, that act did not trigger tears; it comforted me. A week later, at Christmas, Steve and I drove to Cathy's house, a nearly three-hour drive to Grass Valley in the foothills of the Sierras. Cathy and Randy had built a new home, which John knew about, but didn't live to see. It was healing to be with the family and, especially, to see the joy of the great-grandchildren as they opened presents. All of Cathy's children were with us. We ate and drank and felt blessed to have one another.

Despite not feeling a whole person, I was acting as if I were a whole person, driving places, going on trips, joining in on holiday celebrations. I was beginning to trust that becoming whole again—leaving the grieving process behind—would happen if I just kept going forward.

I had visited Pat and Dom in late October and showed them the pictures I had taken in Venice. Though both were happy to see me, Dom said he was not feeling very well, but was resigned to feeling poorly. Their son, a noted sculptor from Montreal, had visited. Their daughter Donna, who lives in the area, was there frequently. By this time, Hospice was in the house. It was hard to visit; Pat, in her dementia, was unable to communicate fully, and Dom was not going to get well. I felt grief edging its way into me again. Still, every time I went to their home, I came away with a feeling that the visit was deeply appreciated. If there was grief, there was also love among us.

When Dom was told he was dying, Donna called and asked me to talk to him. I had had some talks with Dom during other difficult periods and had used, then, my training as a counselor to help him see how much good he had done in his life. Now, Donna wanted me to help ease her father's fear of dying. I didn't know if I could do that, but I went in to see him. He was slumped down on his bed.

"I hear you're dying," I said.

"Yeah." He stretched out the word, regret in having to acknowledge his fate coming through his tone.

"How do you feel about it?" I waited for an answer.

"It's not so much dying that frightens me. It's the actual act of dying," he confessed. "I don't know what to expect."

So I sat, holding his hand, sharing with him the scene at John's deathbed. I told him how John had held fast to my hand or the hand of one of his children or his grandchildren as we waited with him. I told Dom how John couldn't talk anymore but managed to whisper, "I love you." to those who put their ears to his mouth. I described how peaceful John seemed with the morphine doing its job, and with all of us talking to him—reading from his book on his trek across the country during his youth, or telling him not to be afraid of the journey he was taking now. Dom listened intently.

"Yeah," he kept saying, and the tone in his voice became increasingly appreciative and then comforted.

I told him that, in the end, none of us had been with John as he died at 3:20 in the morning, and when we responded to the call to come, we saw John, still deceptively warm, with a very satisfied smile on his face. In life, that smile had meant he understood something. I knew he, at last, understood what I eventually would come to know at the end of my own life.

"When your time comes, Dom. You'll be ready," I told him. We hugged each other and began to talk about the good times we had experienced together and even the common environment that John and he had shared in New

York City as first-generation immigrant Italian children. The talk brought on laughter, and soon Dom was calling for his nurse to come and bring the wheelchair. He was going to sit up and watch television in the den.

In November, I was invited to Dom's 89th birthday. He was delighted to have his daughter, her family, a cherished caregiver, and me at his table. It must have felt somewhat like old times to him, as Dom always loved the fellowship around a good old-fashioned Italian dining table. No matter that this was a kitchen table; the fellowship was quite real. As I was leaving, Pat stopped me and surprised me with a clear expression, "You married?" I explained that I was partnered with John and that he had died. She looked puzzled and then said, "John?" as if she suddenly remembered him. "Yes, John," I repeated. "John died." She shook her head angrily. "Damn!" she said. *Exactly*, I thought.

Chapter Eight:
A Class in Theodicy
(2009)

In the first year after John died, I found myself longing for relief from sudden tears, impatient for a feeling of joy to manifest itself and stay with me—not just visit me in brief spurts and vanish as quickly as it comes, leaving me alone once again to feel empty and troubled by constant neediness. At times, grief felt shameful, self-indulgent, unworthy of the attention of my friends and family. I didn't want to bother others with my grief and didn't fully appreciate that others were bothered, not so much by my grieving, but by their own helplessness in comforting me.

We aren't taught how to talk about death in our youth-oriented society. Sometimes I think that death is a tragic inconvenience made endurable by our funeral rituals that give us organized and predictable closure. Those who mourn with us at such times have comforting words to say, a hug, a memory, and a sincere invitation to call upon them if there is anything at all they can do. Those kind acts fulfill a prescribed obligation and provide closure to sympathizers;

we who are left with grief experience the long aftermath of loss as neither organized nor predictable.

Why do we have to grieve anyway? Isn't it enough that our loved one has safely left life and is no longer suffering? Why did God invent suffering or does he, or she or whoever is in charge of the universe, simply turn a blind eye to events that cause suffering? Atheists dismiss the idea of a God existing, many arguing that if there were such a powerful force, he or she would not allow evil things to happen in the world. Why doesn't God intervene when evil things happen?

My questions are universal ones. In a course formally known as theodicy, seminarians study such issues, asking where God is when evil things happen and why he doesn't prevent evil or events that cause human suffering. Perhaps all who grieve need a class in theodicy.

As the New Year approached, I found myself fingering a large lamb roast in Costco. With the effervescent enthusiasm that given a new slate of time each year seems to evoke, I felt exhilarated at being safely past a year of grieving. Surely it was time to declare an end to grief and move on. I bought the roast and invited my friends to a New Year's dinner party.

Art, Maureen's husband, brought wine for those who cared to drink it, and I supplied sparkling apple juice for the rest of us. Helga and her husband Morey brought a cake, Anne brought a pink cyclamen to decorate the table, and Myra, whose husband by now was in a nursing home, brought her optimistic spirit. These were my closest friends: women from the Wednesday morning group and their mates; people who were glad to share my joy at the prospect of a whole new year buoyed with hope, not only for me, but for themselves as well.

We ate, we drank, we toasted. We sat and contemplated America's first African-American president and were proud to be part of that historic moment. We discussed the worsening economy, the alarming number of failed home loans, which gave rise to the recession we were experiencing. We agreed on causes for the failures, but not on remedies. All of us had opinions on taxes, particularly on California's property taxes, which are restricted under Proposition 13, passed into law years ago. We had no effective answers to the national crises, but it wasn't for lack of trying.

On a personal level, I was worried about finances. The money John left me was invested in the stock market and all of it disappeared, at least on paper, as the stock market fell. I experienced, as did many in the rest of the country, a 30% loss in my modest portfolio. Perhaps if I had known we were going into recession, I would not have spent the money to go to Venice. A widow, traditionally, loses income when her spouse dies. In my case, because John and I were domestic partners, I wasn't able to collect his social security, a loss of nearly $1,000 a month. (Domestic partners are viewed as married in California, but not by the federal government.) After his death, I budgeted even more closely, forgoing luxuries like pedicures and looking for bargains when shopping in the grocery store. Unexpected expenses in the form of treatment for subterranean termites and multi-thousand dollar dental work threw me into panic mode. Yet, like the federal government, I have learned to live with deficits.

I count my blessings, a home and car that I own free and clear, some money in the portfolio and the ability to budget. I was taught that skill in college and have been grateful for it ever since. Saving is second nature to me. I stretch my dollars, and though I can be generous, I am careful about spending money. I also take advantage of any program that offers discounts based on low-income for, without John's input, my income qualified as low. My assets are generally unavailable for expenses as invested assets generate the income I use for living expenses. I'm lucky to have assets. It's quite a change to accept a restrained standard of living, but because of the recession, I am not alone. Unfortunately, young families have felt the sting, some losing their jobs and homes. By comparison, I am rich indeed.

As my friends and I debated the financial woes of the country, I felt a sense of relief. Being able to intellectualize such loss and participate in the discussion was a sign to me that, though the country might be falling apart, my life was finally coming together in a logical normalcy.

Normalcy lasted six days. The first Tuesday after New Year's Day, Dom died. Two days later I called Marion and caught her just as she was getting home from a visit to her doctor. He had given her six months to live and was calling in Hospice. *Why? It didn't make sense. After all that she had gone through and had survived, why now was she dying?* I could get no satisfactory answer from her or her husband or even my younger sister, who, while still not talking to me, had agreed to email me about Marion.

Marion told me she wasn't eating. She just didn't feel like eating she said. If one doesn't eat, one eventually dies. A churchgoer, Marion had a strong belief in God, so I asked her if she wanted to see God. "No," she said. "No?" I asked, surprised at her answer. "I'm just not ready to die," she said.

"Well, live then," I said. "Fight it."

Grief came rushing back. Dom's death brought tears not only for him, but for John and for the life we all had shared. That part of life was irretrievably over; even sharing bittersweet memories with Dom was gone. Added to that grief was the stress of having another death to face, a precious sister, a precious link to my childhood about to be broken and a younger sister no longer willing to be in a meaningful relationship with me.

I dared not open the Pandora box of grief that being estranged from my older son and his family triggered.

Knowing that I was about to become a great-grandmother by Mike's oldest, Kimberly, and that there was a good chance I'd never meet this new child, only sharpened the loss of Dom, the impending loss of Marion, and the loss of my relationship with Flo.

How do families get into these terrible situations? In my case, my future daughter-in-law ignored me from the beginning. The day we met, she talked to my mother, to Mike, to my other son Steve, and even to a visiting friend, but had little to say to me. Later, as I tried to develop a relationship with her, she found any suggestion I'd make unappealing and intrusive. She and Mike seldom visited after they married. There were times she refused to talk to me, and so Mike stopped speaking to me as well. She would never identify what I had done to offend her and wasn't interested in my asking for forgiveness. When I asked if we could please have a relationship, she flatly told me she didn't want a relationship with me. After the grandchildren arrived, she'd often have cards and gifts I'd send returned to me by the post office marked "refused."

Since my estrangement with Mike, I have heard many stories of estrangements of sons and daughters from their birth families or from a father or a mother in the family. I know that my situation isn't unique, but I also know, after very many attempts at reconciliation and rebuffs, that the situation is probably hopeless. For my own sanity, I had to give up trying.

I spoke to Tim, our pastor, about my many griefs. He prayed with me and asked me to trust God. I wanted to. I wanted to trust God, and, at times, I felt I could. The Sunday after Dom's death, I went to church. As soon as we began to sing the Kyrie—"Lord have mercy"—tears started rolling down my cheek. Every time we sang anything, the tears rolled. When we shared the peace, Tim gave me a huge hug and whispered that if anyone deserved peace that day it was me.

Later that week, I went to a dinner Donna hosted in memory of her father. I brought a chocolate cake and a written eulogy for Dom. His family had come from Southern California and from Canada to gather around the table in his memory, eat good food, drink good wine, and remember the life Dom and Pat had created for them. As we embraced after I read my eulogy, I felt a surge of warmth and love even from the family members I had just met there. Their histories were familiar to me for Pat had been a member of our Wednesday women's group before her dementia took her from us and, while still coherent, had proudly shared their many accomplishments.

The bad news kept coming. By the middle of February Marion's husband reported that Marion was in the process of dying and that it would probably be "a couple of days." I kept calling. Sometimes I would be able to talk with Marion and she would tell me again that she just wasn't ready. I prayed and I cried. I felt helpless.

I considered flying back to the east coast to see her. The trip would be an expensive one, involving renting a car and driving 150 miles from the airport to her hometown in Delaware. Once there, I would need to stay in a bed and breakfast establishment; I couldn't stay with my younger sister. In the end, I decided not to go, remembering that I had visited only a year and a half earlier and we three sisters had enjoyed a happy time together.

At that precious time we sat as a privileged trio, alone together by Marion's neighbors' pool, laughing at memorable moments of trips in childhood and the foibles of our parents. We shared our childhood hurts and felt healed, for we validated occurrences we weren't free to discuss with one another as children. We teased one another about our ideas of aging; and we felt warm with love for one another.

Having survived and shared adversity as well as joy in life, we were fully bonded and felt that bond in that magical visit.

Better to leave that good memory intact. There was nothing physical I could do for Marion since that was being done, and she had not asked me to come. Neither had her husband.

We've all been trained to value family. Our images of the good life are much like Dom's Italian dinner table where family gathers and toasts each other's health and happiness. Because of these rosy pictures, we expect so much of one another that we sometimes set up our own heartbreaks when reality intrudes.

Long ago I learned to temper my expectations of my family, but I didn't learn to temper my expectations of myself. I have always tried to fix things. When our mother and father argued, I was there in the middle trying to help them sort things out. I was as effective at that as the nagging fly that finally gets swatted away so that the business at hand can continue. I suspect that meddling in my older son's life and in my younger sister's life, when I thought I was being of help, has been a factor in our estrangements.

Now, facing fresh griefs, I was learning once more that there are things I cannot change. I can only change myself and, even then, there is just a limited amount of change to myself I can accomplish on my own. As I was taught in my twelve-step program, I had to turn to a higher power for help.

Tim and I put Marion's name on the prayer list for church. He prayed for her. I prayed for her. She was on the prayer list of her own church, and I'm sure that her many friends and other family members prayed for her as well.

Marion didn't die in February. She began to eat more and seemed to feel better. When I told her we were praying for her, she said, "Don't stop."

I didn't stop, but I was more and more discouraged. I couldn't stop my own grieving. I thought of all the losses in my life and I felt overwhelmed. I knew I couldn't burden Tim and my friends with endless grief talk, so I decided to go for professional counseling. I couldn't fix anything in my life; I needed fixing. Six sessions later, I was reconstituted. I learned to detach with love, a concept that I was familiar with from still another twelve-step program I had attended earlier in life. I saw the ones I loved as separate people with whom I could sympathize and comfort, if allowed, but whom I needed to respect as agents of their own life happenings. Thus, for instance, both my younger sister and I could exist as persons in our own rights, not subject to judgment and criticism from one another, but accepted as we were.

Hadn't I learned that useful concept in my 74 years of living? Of course, but sometimes the things we learn tend to slip away from us, especially when we feel threatened. I felt better, stabilized emotionally.

Towards the end of March, Marion had a seizure and was admitted to the Hospice Center where they expected her to die within four days. I alerted Steve who was to travel with me to the East Coast when she died. We kept praying. Marion didn't die. After her allotted four days were over, she was transferred to a nursing home where she received intensive care through April, and towards the end of May, she was transferred to an assisted living facility. In June, she came home. She is our miracle. She is a testament to the power of prayer and to the mercy of God.

Marion's unexpected recovery brought a cautious relief to me. I felt grateful and was especially aware that church members were happy for me. I didn't feel exactly comfortable, however. I was still a newcomer in church, still learning the ins and outs of the organization and wondering where or whether I fit in. Again, the shame I felt in having so much grief come into my life made me wonder whether people saw only that part of me, not the whole person I so wanted to be.

I decided it was time to do something about it. I called the pastor and asked for a home visit. Tim knew the needy person in me, but not much about the rest of me. We had a pleasant visit. At one point, I escorted him through my house and talked about the origins of the many paintings and photographs on the walls and on tables and dressers. As I talked about the images, I began to get memories of what was happening in my life at the times I acquired the pieces for my collection. Like an old-fashioned camera coming into surprising focus, I suddenly recognized the history that grounds me. In sharing some of that history with Tim, I was becoming real as much to myself as to Tim. Life wasn't just about grief anymore.

We sat and talked about his ministry. Since I am on the TIM advisory committee—where Tim encourages feed-back—with his permission, I offered an observation based on comments I had heard from church members. I told him that he is excellent in his writing, a learned scholar, and a very good preacher. I suggested that he has what I called a "growing edge," which I described as a space to learn more about teaching and group management in his Bible classes. I chose my words carefully, wanting to be gentle, non-judgmental. Tim nodded and said that he appreciated my feedback, but when he left, I again felt as if I had gone too far. That Sunday his homily was on strengths and weaknesses and, without identifying its source, he mentioned my feedback as part of an "otherwise lovely visit."

"Bothered you a bit," I said, smiling, when I hugged him while sharing the peace. He grinned, admitting it did. "But you got a great sermon from it," I said. I really like Tim's willingness to use his own humanity as an example in his preaching to the congregation. He knows he has feet of clay just like the rest of us, but he also knows he is a child of God; he is accomplished in showing us we are God's children as well.

Coincidental to my grieving and suffering, Tim planned a Wednesday night Bible class in theodicy to start after Easter. Theodicy, he explained in the Sunday bulletin, is a study of whether and why God allows evil and suffering in the world. The class seemed tailor-made for me and I planned to be a participant.

As I thought about my critique of his teaching and group management skills, I was struck with an enticing idea. Once more I would step forward with support for Tim, this time with action rather than words. I am a retired schoolteacher and a trained therapist with experience in facilitating groups. I called Tim and asked if I could help him teach the class. He accepted without reservation. "Let's meet next week and go over my notes."

We met in the library of the church. Tim gave me his outline for the class and explained what he hoped to accomplish. As he talked, I was able to see rich possibilities in our collaboration. I suggested the class meet in a circle; Tim wanted a table for his materials. We compromised on an area of small tables that formed a square big enough for eight to ten people to congregate, yet easily see one another and interact comfortably. I suggested we needed an introduction exercise, for participants may not know one another as well as we hoped. He put me in charge of that. Then we planned the first class, one that would reveal different images of God held by class members.

We talked together about our own images of God and what we might expect to hear from others. As we continued to talk of God, suffering, and evil, a strange feeling engulfed me, strange only because I had forgotten the feeling. A joyful aliveness, a kind of spring-has-sprung-and-the-whole-world's-in-bloom realization washed over me. My intellect was being reactivated. Familiar concepts flooded my thoughts. The promise of meeting a fresh challenge, in teaching and learning once more, chased out of my mind memories of the emotional turmoil that had worn me down. I was making another important turn in my life.

Chapter Nine:
The Spirit Moves Me
(2009)

I remember sitting with my classmates in Miss Owens's fifth grade room when the sky turned dark as night shortly after lunch. Wind and rain rattled and pelted the windows, beating a frightening tandem rhythm in our ten-year-old hearts. Periodically, the door opened and someone's parent scooped up a child, saving him or her from the developing hurricane's fury. What would happen to me? My father was at work and my mother didn't drive. Would all the other parents come, leaving me alone to battle fruitlessly with rain, wind and all-consuming darkness to come to who knew what devastating and terrible end—alone, alone, so all alone?

The door opened again, and there stood my father, calling me to rush into his waiting arms. I ran to him, my heart bursting with surprise and happiness, and breathed in the warm sweet father smell of his comforting body. The familiar fragrance mingled pleasantly with aromas of the rich pipe tobacco he smoked and his Old Spice shaving lotion.

He shifted me to the protection of his right arm, under his overcoat; on his left was my younger sister. The two of us pressed hard against him like chicks under a mother's wing. As we braved the elements, it was our father who was hit by the pelting rain and sturdy wind, but he knew his way in the darkness, walking us straight to his waiting car. Inside, my sister and I curled up on the back seat, safe in the softness of upholstery that smelled of popcorn and candy from happy movie-going trips, and just a little of the tobacco smoke, and maybe a trace of fish he'd caught in the river and carted to neighbors.

Our father drove while we delighted in our security. Nothing, *nothing* now would harm us. We were his daughters, and he had come to carry us home to our mother with her own sweet smell of nurturing body and offerings of vegetable soup, homemade cinnamon rolls and a steaming cup of cocoa. The road was a river of wet and darkness with tree branches bouncing unexpectedly in our path and, sometimes, a power line or two, which Dad maneuvered around. We didn't notice. We didn't have to. We were under his care and protection.

This was my God, a ten-year-old's notion of what God not only should be, but was—a caring, loving protector who comes for me when I am alone and frightened, who shelters me as he braves wind, rain and darkness, who drives an unerring course to the safety of home and a mother's sweet care. This is the God I've always wanted, the God I want today—someone who cares enough to look for me in trouble, who offers protection and guides me safely home to the warmth of his nurturing self—a God who loves me so much I cannot perish, a God whose good-father smell is instantly recognizable, instantly comforting and secure.

I did not sustain the faith of that ten-year-old. As I grew, I began to see the faults in my father: He was old, I was young; he knew nothing; I knew everything. Part of this distancing was a natural growth process, a separation that allowed me to become an individual with power of my own. I needed to learn how to live safely in the world, experiencing the effects of adverse conditions, surviving them, and then applying lessons learned to create a life for myself. In essence, I became my own god.

I also became aware of the inadequacies of religion. In my early twenties I led a small youth group in my hometown Methodist church. When Mr. Dee, a powerful church leader, heard that I allowed the youngsters to dance in the church basement, he confronted me. To him, dancing was a sin; I was told to stop encouraging youth to sin. I protested, saying I'd bring the issue up in church, but Mr. Dee warned that, by getting others involved, I would split the church! I blanched. My innocent youth could not bear such a burden. On the other hand, I didn't care much for a god who didn't dance. It simply didn't make sense that providing fun for youngsters who, left on their own devices, could find far more harmful mischief to get into, was a sin.

As the "thou shalt nots" became more evident, I moved away from God, appalled that I could never live up to the restrictions of commandments, especially as interpreted by the sanctimonious among us. I was repelled and still am, for the most part, by people who have such a strict moral code that offenders are criticized and condemned out-of-hand, without regard or pity for the human flaws in all of us.

I did cling to my own idea of a loving, protective God, however, because I needed that image to cope with life. It was only after marriage and the realities of motherhood and responsibilities as a lonely Navy wife began to suffocate my own dreams—of who I wanted to be and what I wanted to accomplish—that I began to drink seriously. Intoxicating spirits gave me a sense of individuality and worth. With the freedom alcohol provided, I could indulge in grandiose fantasies, imagining myself as a famous and loved author, sought after for my views and insights. For a little while, I could believe that my life mattered.

As I progressed in my drinking, my fantasies became more personal. I saw myself as a femme fatale and acted on my fantasies. At the time, I never appreciated the danger and shame that course would bring to me. Eventually, I became very ill with classic signs of alcoholism.

It was a loving and protective God that came to me, in my 38th year of life, as I lay helpless on my own couch after a nightmarish weekend of threatening dreams, hallucinations, and paranoia that made me sure I was losing my mind. I stared at a painting of Tahiti on my living room wall, and in the colors of the sunset, two figures emerged. The Virgin Mary in her blue cowl was cradling the head of a crucified Jesus. I can still see that image faintly today, but back then, in my fear and despair, the image was sharp and clear, quietly there for me. "I don't believe in you," I said, "but you are sure better than what I have been seeing."

It took many years of being in a twelve-step program before I could acknowledge that I, not only believed in God, but depended on him to keep me sane and sober.

When I joined Tim's class on theodicy, I came with a simple belief in God. I saw Him as a multi-dimensional being, both distant and personal—a being that ran the universe and my life. Now, the measure of my belief is changing. As I participated in that first class with Tim, I found that I still had much to learn about God and the way he works within me. Like the rest of the class, I began writing in my journal.

An entry, from an early session of the class, surprised me: "My God is forever bringing me out of crises. Minor or major, he is there for me. It is I who can't seem to walk in His Love in perfect trust and harmony. It seems impossible. The only way to do it is: to stay in the moment, live for today—let the past go and refuse to live in the future. A lot of trust is used in being present: trust that there is sufficiency in the present and trust that the future is forever waiting."

I was not in the habit of affirming God's presence and the way he works with me, yet journal entries like this seemed to flow effortless from my pen. Even more surprising was the happiness I felt in writing these comments. Week after week I'd share a journal entry that inspired even me. My colleagues in the class made comments on the beauty of the writing. Suddenly, I became aware of myself and felt embarrassed. I told Tim I sensed the way I expressed myself in writing was being appreciated, rather than the ideas I was advancing.

"I know how you feel," he told me. "The same thing happened to me in seminary in creating homilies." He talked to his professor and was given advice he passed on to me: "You have a gift," he said. "Don't denigrate the gift that was given to you. Use it." I relaxed. Soon I was sharing my journal entries with ease.

Since the journal entries felt inspired, I considered them a gift that came through me, entries that I was not only to share, but also entries from which I was meant to learn. Therapists assign journaling exercises to their clients to bring them awareness and insight on their troublesome issues. As a therapist, I've made such assignments myself, so wouldn't a spiritual journal bring enlightenment to the spirit?

As obvious as some of my conclusions were, to me these insights felt as if they were completely new. The renewal of my spirit from the depths of my grieving brought me back into a world where intellect was once again valued; coupled with belief, there was freshness to life now that gave me a measure of certainty and joy.

Our class was small with participants coming and going throughout the spring and summer sessions. Discussions were lively and ideas fully explored. We didn't worry about heresy or proper Christian attitudes. Our views ranged from traditional to radical beliefs, but all of us were believers.

We read Elie Wiesel's *Night*, a harrowing account of his imprisonment and treatment in Nazi concentration camps, when just a teenager during World War II. We struggled to understand, not so much Wiesel's loss of faith in a God who seemed absently indifferent to such evil, but why some Jews still prayed in spite of unbearable pain and hardship.

We experienced the drama of the Creation and fall in the book of Genesis and wondered whether God was responsible for human suffering. Who, after all, put the Tree of the Knowledge of Good and Evil in the Garden of Eden? Was the fall the fault of Adam who was dumb enough to listen to his wife when she offered him a bite of the apple? Or was the fault in the woman, Eve—the woman God had given him Adam reminded God—thus making the fault God's again? Or was the cause of human suffering the serpent forever seen as evil, one who fostered temptation and rebellion?

In later sessions, we considered that God himself might suffer, that we live with a fragile God in a fragile world. In this view God sees the suffering and asks the question of us—why don't *you* do something about it? Humans are in charge of their world and have freedom to make choices; humans are not puppets of God.

Tim and I would meet on the day after each class to review the session and plan the next week's session. These planning sessions were joyful. There was something at work in them besides two educated humans discussing ideas and strategies for sharing these ideas with the class. We both felt energized and refreshed after a session. We were blessed to have one another and we both acknowledged that blessing and gave the credit to God.

For me, there was something else happening that was delightful and disturbing. I felt a deep love for Tim. It probably was inevitable that, after having lost my beloved John, I would someday again feel love for another male, but I neither expected nor wanted to feel that way about someone who was helping me rediscover myself. My relationship with Tim was too valuable for love! I felt conflicted.

Please God, I prayed, *I don't want to love Tim.* How short-sighted I was—but, as I realized before, I still had much to learn. We are conditioned to believe that love is romantic. Love for one's children and love for one's friends of the same gender (unless one is gay and in love) is a different kind of love than love for another of the opposite gender. I got caught up in that conditioning, and though I knew that there are different kinds of love, I was frightened by the idea that I might harbor some forbidden attraction to Tim. The only way to deal with this was for me to continue to pray about my dilemma, and I did.

Soon, I was able to analyze my feelings. Being older and being without a partner, after having had traditional romantic love relationships all my adult life, is bewildering. I've had enough of the relationship games men and women play, and I am no longer interested in the kind of sexual experiences I had in my youth. If I want a romantic relationship, I really only want to feel a love and closeness with a partner near my age and life experience, ideally someone who has fully dealt with any grief issues he may have. I'm not even sure I want that! I am so fully engaged in learning about living alone, being responsible to and for myself, that I don't want to be interrupted, just now, with the responsibilities romantic love brings. If lack of love and closeness is the price for that life choice, so be it.

That Sunday in greeting Tim after the service, I felt such joy, such gratitude for life, that I told Tim, "I love you."

"What a nice thing to say," he said as he hugged me. "Thank you. I love you, too." And that was it. That was the answer to my prayer. My fear of loving Tim dissolved in the realization that we were sharing what God offered, a love based in spirituality, the same kind of love I feel for people who are in my twelve-step program, people who are on a common journey with me. Tim, six years younger than my younger son, was resettled in my mind as my pastor, a kind of father figure to me in his role, a loving guide who loves me the same way I love him. I am fortunate in moving beyond my twelve-step program into a wider community, one that is offering me a deeper understanding not only of myself but also of the greatest of human values, love.

By now I was also realizing that there is a force within me, loving me and showing me how to live a full and abundant life once again. In my lifetime I have resisted the idea of a Holy Spirit as a guide, but, needing to believe something was guarding and guiding me, I've been attracted to the idea of guardian angels. Like many others who are cautious about organized religion, I wanted more out of life. I wanted a connection to a Higher Power that makes the sky blue and brings ocean waters to shore in foaming, dancing bubbles. I wanted reassurance of a life beyond life, but I wanted none of the "thou shalt nots" of organized religion. Talking about the Holy Spirit would have been embarrassment akin to taking leave of my rational self to wander among the vocally righteous and their sanctimonious certainties about God.

Yet this experience of the spirit within me was different. Ideas that made sense came easily to me, ideas that I wanted to explore and use, ideas that I indeed *chose* to explore and use. I could have easily rejected those ideas, but then I would have been on my own again, struggling with the issues of grief and loss in my life, rather than being surrounded with affirmations and love.

As if my spirit knew I needed another human being to lavish my loving concern on, I was attracted in a twelve-step meeting to a young woman who was grieving the loss of her mother. When I approached her after the meeting, she spoke of being isolated in her grief, and I was moved to suggest to her that she needed in her life something spiritual.

I invited her to our Bible study, and she came to the classes. She and I share our experiences of grief and recovery and we have grown close. We are friends.

One of the readings Tim assigned in the class was a chapter, "Conditions of Prayer" from *In God's Presence*, a book written by Marjorie Suchochi. Divine guidance, Suchochi says, "is more like an impulse toward the best responsiveness to whatever our situation might be." The impulse may not be conscious, she says, but "we experience its effects." I believe that, at present, I am blessed with the consciousness of that impulse; its effects, in my writing and work with others, demonstrate the divine guidance I receive in bringing out the best in myself and others.

In my journal the day that we read Suchochi, I wrote: "The idea that God has a freely chosen character is new to me. It's as if God can change—can adapt to different circumstances and different people so that all comes together through Him. Suchochi says God does this and then gives "consequent possibility back to us as an impulse for good."

There is happiness in gaining knowledge of oneself through the work of educators and scholars. Tim has provided me an opportunity to nourish my spirit through study, through planning classes with him, and through teaching and learning with the materials he has introduced to me. More than the pure joy of it all, is the astounding realization that life makes sense when seen through the prism of a renewed faith in God and the shared experience of seeking to understand the workings of the mind of God. Perhaps life and death and God Himself are mysteries, felt but not easily explained. Yet, I find exhilarating the freedom to raise questions and explore the possibilities of what life, death and God might be.

One of the questions Tim asked of us was how we viewed the Bible in its capacity to deliver the word of God.

"Humans need their stories," this journal entry began. "Cave dwellers drew their stories on the walls of their caves: stories that left a record for others to see and interpret; stories that gave instruction, perhaps of the hunt or food gathering; and stories that inspired others to action. The Bible is a continuation of telling our stories. Our need to explain is as simple as a child's question: Where did I come from? Our puzzlement over the meaning of life and whether our lives survive after death defines our need for explanation. The Bible is a collection of books that provide answers within a Judeo-Christian context. For me, the universal truths within the Bible, the general principles of good and evil and the Love of God, make the Bible a holy text and outweigh any conflicts in details."

An idea, a glimmer of meaning, penetrated as I continued to write: "Life makes no sense without God who keeps an orderly universe. I have a deep trust that such order is a constant reflected in the Bible. The historical aspect is in God's word for a specific time, and some of the statements make sense only in a historical context. Maybe this view presents a dilemma, in that I can choose what is relevant to life as it is now and ignore what seems outdated. Yet, the word of God in the Bible is ever evolving. Meaning comes to me as I am ready for its revelation. So, yes, the Bible delivers the word of God today, as effectively as it did when it was first written." It was satisfying for me to write these words even as I knew mine was an argument open to challenge.

When, in class, we reached the concept of personal suffering, there was a shift in my feelings. I was depressed. I realized that the grief I had been experiencing was a form of suffering, but I had deliberately inhibited myself from going beneath that grief to that deeper place where I store that long-held sorrow of the fourteen years my older son has not spoken to me. "Some of my intense suffering," I finally wrote in my journal, "has been my pain over rejection by my older son and the loss of seeing my grandchildren." Tears spotted the paper. "I did not suffer in silence. I have tried to break through this awful shunning by asking for forgiveness even though I didn't know just how I offended. I tried to communicate, but suffered further when letters and packages I'd mailed came back refused. Finally, I started praying for my son and his wife, a concept taught me in my twelve-step program. I asked that peace and happiness be given them. Only the praying has worked, allowing me to release them to the care of God."

Still, the pain is with me and is especially sharp when news and pictures of Mike and his family go to my sisters and to my ex-husband's family, but not to me.

I have worked at coping with this pain. Mostly, I keep it tucked in a safe place in my solar plexus, which I call a pain pocket. Once in awhile, I take the pain from that pocket, feel it, and put it back again. This revisiting happens sometimes when my friends talk joyfully of their grandchildren, and I have little in that area to share—notwithstanding that John shared *his* grandchildren with me, one of whom I was lucky enough to love from the start of his life.

So when, in the class, Tim asked how we experience suffering, I did not read my journal entry. The pain itself surfaced. I couldn't just *read*. From the depths of my despair, I poured out my suffering, shedding tears as I talked. My classmates listened. I could feel them experiencing anew their own suffering, suffering triggered by the telling of mine.

As I paused, they began to share their experiences, their own hurts by loved ones, and I knew I was not alone. When human beings, who should be close to us, hurt us, we suffer pain that often cannot be alleviated. There is no understanding for infliction of such pain, just acceptance.

I learned once again to pray for the well-being of my son and his family, so I could make a kind of peace with my pain, an agreement that the pain will ordinarily stay in its designated pocket permitting me to live my life mostly unattached to that pain.

I felt more comfortable when we intellectualized suffering, looking at its four dimensions as described by Douglas John Hall in his book, *God and Human Suffering: A Exercise in the Theology of the Cross.* Hall identifies these dimensions as loneliness, temptation, anxiety, and limitation. Limitation is what I have in my relationship with my older son. I cannot reach beyond the barrier presented to me. To have a realistic understanding of this limitation is comforting.

There are, of course, unimaginable human sufferings. The sufferings we experience in our Western society seem, to use Hall's words, "luxurious by comparison." Who can bear the faces and the swollen bellies of the hungry children of the world that we find impossible to feed adequately? We suffer helplessness and turn away. Even though we know pain because we have felt pain, we often cannot face the pain of others.

When the class had talked enough about the agonies of suffering, we began to examine the possibility that God, himself, suffers. Theologian and novelist Frederick Buechner in his essay "Walking in the World with a Fragile God" believes God wept when terrorists in planes brought down the World Trade Center on September 11, 2001. He wept with suffering families of the dead and with all of us in the United States who were weeping and with those weeping in countries beyond. Suffering, Buechner reminds us, is at the heart of what love is. For if we love, as God loves us, we suffer when suffering comes to loved ones.

What takes a leap of faith for some, but for me feels undeniable, is that no matter what form our suffering takes, God is with us. I think that God has been with me throughout my grieving even when I wasn't conscious of His presence. I know that I have been spiritually moved to a new appreciation of my life by taking part in the class in theodicy.

The spirit moved me in yet another way. One day while looking through files on my computer, I found the essay I had written earlier in life called "The Stranger in Me." Impulsively, I shared it with my neighbor. I also brought Vera some of my journal writings and shared them. She identified with many of my feelings and excitedly declared, "You have to write a book."

The idea excited me as well. Could I really have something to say to others, particularly to people my age that are experiencing increasing losses in their lives? In the same solar plexus where my pocket of grief resides, excitement was bubbling. I felt nudged, yes, psychically, emotionally, and intellectually nudged by the Holy Spirit. I knew. I just knew I could and would write this book.

Chapter Ten:
A Real Life
(2009)

A day after the second anniversary of John's death, I attended a winter holiday open house at my bank, a perk that comes with living in a community for seniors. Though I had attended the same party last year, this year was different. Last year I was still too uncertain of myself to really socialize. I felt awkward, a wallflower among the many couples there, but this year I was more at ease.

The first person I talked to was a widow of 18 months. "You never get over it," she assured me.

"It *is* hard," I agreed in part, "but you have to rebuild your life."

"At my age!" she retorted. "Oh, no, that's impossible."

I wanted to tell her about my experiences, but already she was moving away from me. No one was going to mess with her grief, I could tell.

A neighbor greeted me. "How are you?"

I told her I was doing well, and that yesterday I had lit a candle on the anniversary of John's death. She expressed her sympathy and we talked about the book I was writing. She was happy to see me in a positive frame of mind.

After a few more encounters with widows and women who lived alone, I made small talk with a man. "Did you taste the shrimp? Good, isn't it?" I began.

"Yes," he agreed. "It's nice the bank builds good relationships with these parties."

"Yes it is. I've had three good relationships myself," I ventured, thinking God knows what except that the thought slipped from my mind to my mouth.

"Well, I've only had one," he said. His eyes drifted to his wife standing across the counter between us. There were a lot of good-looking senior men in the crowd, but a wife, nearby, would miraculously materialize the minute I started to talk to one of them. Protocol, I sensed, was to talk to the wife, and so I did, introducing myself, asking her name and her husband's, and adding, quickly and emphatically, that I greatly admire long-standing marriages, which is the truth. I was acutely aware, however, that I felt like, and probably was viewed as, a stalking shark ready to devour relationships. If only my mouth would refrain from casting out the suggestive thoughts of a person hungry for attention. I have no illusions or designs that I could intrude on the relationships of others. Despite the reported penchant of men for other women, husbands and wives of our ages are pretty much embedded with one other, made one by the intricacies of many years, as it should be. Old habits die hard, however, and most wives are wary of widows, especially ones who approach their men.

I remember a dinner party in Hawaii when John caught the eye of a lively 90-year-old who had come to the party with a young man who looked after her. Barbara was cheerfully flirtatious. She reminded me of my own mother who wasn't a bit shy herself. She kept a conversation going with John, who seemed to be enjoying her, as she was a lively, intelligent woman. Eventually, she told me that she was going to take John home with her.

I was amused because I knew that John was totally dependent on me to manage his life. He was becoming somewhat physically fragile at that point, and I was his caregiver-in-training; he wasn't about to trade me in.

We had a wonderful dinner with our friends, and when it was time to leave, Barbara and her friend made the first move. As she said her goodbyes to us, I said, "Wait a minute, Barbara. You forgot something."

"I forgot something?" she said, puzzled.

"Yes," I said, taking John's hand and offering it to her. "You forgot this."

We laughed. Now, why can't my encounters be as light as that one?

Our job as lonely senior women seems to be to hunt for a new man. "You have to check out the obituaries," I was actually told. "Available men go fast!" Do humans actually do such things? This suggested tactic reminds me of people who reportedly check obituaries in New York City in a quest for rent-controlled apartments.

It does seem that men tend to find new relationships pretty fast. John came to me only four months after Edna died. With women, however, finding a new relationship is not that easy. I suspect that many older widows may be so worn out by their caregiving that they are wary of starting anew with an aged man. I knew one such widow who found love with a man her age and had five or six good years with him. When he got sick, she left him to be cared for by his children and moved closer to her own children. Though the abandonment may be shocking, you've got to admire a woman who takes care of herself.

Another widow friend, who has since died, was quite aggressive in her search for a companion. She met a married man in her church and had a clandestine affair with him. This affair began in her early seventies! She also actually stalked an elderly boyfriend who left her for another woman until I advised her she could be arrested! Such is sex for the seventies crowd.

As for me, I'm not sure what I want. I like men. I like to talk to them and I like to even flirt a little, but I also am beginning to like the independence that has come to me. As my own person, I come and go as I please.

Still, at home at night, the loneliness comes in and I long for someone beside me just to talk with in an intimate way. Intimacy, for me, can be as simple as a conversation about a television program. The important component is that a person is there for me, listening, responding and caring that I exist and that I like being with him.

Every time I walk from my church to the parking lot, I am aware that I am alone. There are other women, like me, who walk from the church alone. Maybe we are going home or out to brunch with more women from the church, the latter choice giving us a destination with connection to others. Still, on the walk to the car there is that tiny moment of acute distress, the feeling that everyone, but me, has a real life. The feeling is totally irrational and is gone the moment I start the car and begin to listen to classical music on the radio.

Yet, the feeling doesn't stay gone; it creeps up on me like a gray sky that suddenly thickens into the kind of darkness that threatens a storm. I push against that feeling. If it happens at home, I jump from my chair and hurry into the kitchen. There I either eat something sweet or switch on the computer to play the games that distract me. If I allow myself, I listen to the spirit within. I turn away from the games and open a document so I can write. On the white space that looks like paper, but isn't, I can begin to confront the feeling that I do have a life, a life that looks real, but isn't.

It's not so much a family that I miss, for I have my son and other relatives, including John's family, with whom I have connection. My church, too, is a family to me. What I don't have is the intimacy of a partner. What is more puzzling and confusing, is I want the intimacy, but I don't know if I want the partner.

I've been going out with a 62-year-old man. We thoroughly enjoy being together, seeing a play or going to the California Academy of Sciences in the city. We are able to easily talk and laugh together. We are friends.

I like him a lot and he likes me. He is old-fashioned in that he opens doors for me and takes my arm to help me out of the car or to avoid hazards while walking. We even hold hands as a gesture of affection and hug in greeting and parting, but beyond that there seems to be no chemistry between us.

I wrestle with myself. *What do you want?* I ask myself. A little male energy has come into my life, and it's enjoyable to have that attention. I think I want more, but the thought of turning a friendship into a romance is weighty.

Rebuilding a life with someone else at twenty, thirty, forty or even fifty seems doable, but at seventy plus? What if the romance becomes serious enough to live together? Where do you live? Who gives up housing that has built-in memories and comfort? What about finances? Who pays for what? What happens to the inheritance you hope to leave to your children?

Earlier in life, I'd turn a semi-blind eye to problems trusting that things would simply work out. Now, I'm not so sure; for with the rich experience of life already lived, I know that choosing a relationship with another involves sacrifice on someone's part—maybe for both individuals.

Then the devil slips into the details: You're too old; you're too fat; you don't even *own* a libido anymore! *Oh yeah?* I fight back with all the bravado I can muster. Yet, there I am squirming with discomfort and going through some sort of senior adolescence, obsessing on my physical limitations and wanting more—just a little more—in life than friendship.

When my friend doesn't call or answer emails, but then pops up, unexpectedly, just as cheerful as ever, asking what will we do next, I get confused. What are we doing? What is this all about anyway?

"Oh, just relax and enjoy the friendship," my friends tell me, and they are right, but my analytical mind seeks a satisfactory resolution. The answer to cooling this somewhat *already cooled* fervor is to say a prayer and admit my own inadequacy in handling this dilemma.

Praying works so well that calm is restored and another thought enters my mind. *This isn't all about you, you know.* The light finally breaks through. My male friend may well have his own demons to wrestle. I am so caught up in my own needs that I have failed to recognize his. We haven't had such deep talks. That sort of conversation is dangerously close to really getting to know one another; neither of us seems inclined to cross the line into this territory.

So, I teeter on the edge of seeking meaningful companionship. The numerous "what ifs" create a solid barrier against risk-taking and keep me safe in my own aloneness; yet being alone deepens loneliness, and loneliness creates anxiety.

Anxiety is a natural part of life. I think it is bred into humans as part of a survival response. Being a little anxious in the primeval jungle made our ancestors pay attention, lest they unwittingly wake a sleeping tiger. In our modern world, our anxieties warn us to be careful in our decisions and actions. Many of us, however, feel anxious when others do not act as we expect them to act. Our minds spin into action inventing stories and excuses either about ourselves or others and we become uncomfortable. Most of us don't like ambiguity.

Obviously the problem of companionship is not mine to work out. With all my thoughts and observations on senior romance, I come back to the reality that one cannot consciously create a meaningful relationship. Again, I learn that I must accept what exists in life rather than what I think life should be.

Taking inventory of my situation and myself, I know that I have attractive qualities. I'm warm and friendly and a good listener. I can be witty and I am generally optimistic and fun to be around. I'm intelligent, can converse knowledgeably on many subjects, and I am open-minded to most ideas. I enjoy my church, classical music concerts, dancing, plays, documentary films that educate and challenge me, movies that make me think, laugh and cry, travel, and projects that allow me to use my intelligence and skills.

My quest then is to live a real life within the qualities given to me. I am in a different phase of life, one without a partner, for now. We live in a coupled world. Many activities, even in church, are designed for couples. I decided not to attend an event in the church, which involved dancing, thinking I'd be despondent watching couples enjoy an activity John and I loved. Afterwards, I talked to a woman friend from church and confessed the reason I hadn't joined the party. "You could have danced with me," she said. Of course, I could have! The single women of the church could have become the life of the party, enjoying the dancing, not bemoaning the lack of a partner!

I'm still learning about real life. My experience, my intuition, and my spiritual faith are protecting me from yielding to impulses that would place me in situations for which I'm not ready. On the other hand I'm beginning to see and appreciate the choices open to me when I widen my view of life. I'm not too old for life. Maybe the secret to living is not to get stuck in old ideas, but to cultivate a willingness to try something new. A new life, perhaps, maybe even a real new life.

Chapter Eleven:
Who Is That Woman?
(2009)

It takes a long time to go through a loved one's personal effects. In the beginning family members were offered choice items of John's. His son-in-law wore a pair of John's shoes to his memorial service, his grandson took his well-loved Timex watch, and a granddaughter was grateful for his bulky silver-gray bathrobe. Other items went to family members and became for me a ritual of shared love, for as much as the items held in memory for me, they were infinitely more valuable to his children and grandchildren.

In the first months after his death, it seemed too soon to take John's clothes out of our closet. I dreaded sorting them. Yet, on occasion, my eye caught a favorite item here and there; I pulled those aside. A soft grey pullover fit me so I wore it a few times, as I did his brown winter coat, which was too snug, yet perfect for imagining his strong arms around me. Flannel shirts I had worn while he was alive, as a buffer against drafts in the house, were equally comforting after his death.

The bulk of the clothes were a problem, however. John used to tease that women stealthily claim closet space until there is barely room for a man's clothes. The truth, in our case, was that John had two closets full of clothes, and it was I who crammed things in the narrow niche he left for me. I confess I took part in creating this problem by buying John many new outfits during our time together, even as he was content with an old, well-worn look.

After he was gone, I'd see his clothes every morning as I dressed—silent, sturdy sentinels waiting for the man who wore them. The man, who once looked so good in them, wore as his last outfit an ordinary hospital nightshirt in which he'd died. Somehow that solid line of clothing took on an unwanted holiness. I couldn't bear the thought of parting with them.

One day when my housecleaners were coming, I opened the closet and starting scooping out armloads of the clothes, hangers and all. Feeling their terrible protesting weight, I hauled them into the spare bedroom and flung them on the bed, choking back the tears that threatened. With steel resolve I went back time after time, indiscriminately gathering whatever was there and piling them in an orderly heap on the bed. Then I shut the doors—the closet, my bedroom and the spare bedroom—and sat down in the living room, heart beating fast.

When the housecleaners came, I told Leticia, the daughter in the team, to take the clothes, hangers and all, out to her car and do whatever she wanted with them. Having a large family, Leticia was delighted to get the clothes, particularly the heavy winter jacket John had worn. Her uncle recently lost his job and had no extra money for the warm jacket he needed. John, I knew, would have been pleased to be of help to the man, and so the act of letting go of his clothes, painful as it was, provided its own small measure of comfort.

There are still odds and ends of clothing left. I don't know why I hold on to them, but I do. There are also drawers full of items like old wallets, leftover hearing aid batteries, small change, eyeglasses, souvenir items, belts, gloves, and other beloved debris he left behind. In time I may spend the change, but just now I can't seem to spill it out of the squeeze top purse he put it in.

When I threw away pairs of false teeth and dental partials he had saved, I shuddered at the personal sense of the act, an eerie echo of losing him. Perhaps that is why it is still so difficult to tackle the work of disposing of anything that was John's.

From his desk, I found old pictures. One of them was of John with a woman I didn't recognize. She was slim and smiling and beautiful. I felt a surge of jealousy, for, obviously, this was a picture taken during our time together. Who was this woman? She was beautiful and seemed so happy with him.

I turned to another picture and the woman was standing next to Ted, my former husband, at a scenic spot in Hawaii! She had on a different outfit, and she looked stunning and happy with him as well.

My mind focused. Incredibly, I was looking at images of myself! Even when I knew that the woman in the pictures was I, I still couldn't believe what I was seeing. I barely remembered the clothes I wore in the photos, let alone my own image!

This younger woman, a couple of years into her fifties, was a stranger to me, the same woman well into her seventies who was writing a book about living with a stranger in herself. It wasn't a case of my brain playing a trick on me. It was truly a moment when I saw myself as other than the ordinary image I have of myself.

I know body image is important to women and has been, probably, since Eve took a bite out of that apple in the Garden of Eden. For a brief time in the 1960s and 1970s feminists tried to assert a woman's body was her own, but women resisted, most of us clinging to our stylized hairdos and makeup and bras, though, gratefully, giving up the confinement of the girdles we had struggled into for years. Alas, today's young women are enticed into the same confinement by garments called body shapers, dissatisfied with their figures, apparently, in the same way we were in our youth.

Body image is a concept so important to women that the beauty industry thrives in the United States even in a recession. There were more than 800,000 American barbers, cosmetologists and personal appearance workers in 2006, according to the U.S. Bureau of Labor Statistics, which also predicts that these jobs will grow faster than the average of all other occupations and increase by 14 percent by 2016.

So when I looked at that stranger in the pictures John had kept in his desk, I knew how thoroughly indoctrinated I'd been to see myself as less than adequate most of the years of my life while, in reality, I was reasonably attractive. This confession is somewhat embarrassing since my advanced degree dissertation was a study of the meaning of a positive experience of the body for women. In that study, I found that women experience their bodies as positive when they make their own choices, acknowledge the benefits of those choices, see themselves as having qualities and affirming them, have the support of other women, and use negativity to illuminate their positive qualities—for instance, modestly disowning a compliment on dress by negating its value as "just an old thing I've had for ages" or, as I have just done, by calling myself "reasonably" attractive.

What it all adds up to is self-esteem, which in many women is in short supply—for our beauty industry keeps us anxious about our looks so that we feel the need to buy the products and use the services they provide. Intellectually,

I know all this. Emotionally? Well, seeing a stranger that in reality was I looking beautiful in an old photo makes me aware that I never saw myself as beautiful and probably never will. I'm like a Pavlov dog, conditioned to respond to the hype that just a little more of a product, or a service, will make a whole lot of difference in my appearance. Only, at my age, I'm less likely to actually buy much beyond lipstick and hair products to create the illusion of beauty.

In reality when I look at people in everyday situations— the store, church, and various meetings I attend—I see individuals who are pleasing to look at. It doesn't matter if someone is overweight or is bald or has skinny legs. I don't see defects. If I do, the first impression is fleeting, as other qualities quickly erase that impression as we begin to talk. I see people who are interesting to talk to or people who move me in some way, making me laugh or stimulating my curiosity about something. Even those I never speak to interest me. I wonder who they are, what they do in life, and whether they have families. If I have an opportunity to quietly observe people, I marvel at the beauty of the human being as a living, breathing creature capable of great acts of kindness and compassion. Only when humans turn into angry, bellowing, self-centered beings or commit terrible acts against one another do I begin to see ugliness. Even then, I seldom attribute their behavior to how their body looks.

So, why would I, beyond a reasonable concern for good grooming, have a poor image of my own body? Maybe I remember when I was a child thinking that old people were unattractive; now *I* have reached the age where children may judge me. As our present population of baby boomers ages, views of older people become more attractive. There is a campaign on television that uses a song, "When I Grow Up I Want to Be an Old Woman" as a plea by a corporate health provider for women to get mammograms. The advertisement is very effective, for it shows older women enjoying life—exercising, dancing, laughing, playing—while the tune beats out the rhythm "an old, old, old, old, old woman." All of the old women are attractive with bodies filled with energy, faces shining with joy or solid contentment—all showing the possibility of being an old woman who loves and is loved by life. The ad is so popular, people find themselves singing the tune and even men have told me: "When I grow up, I want to be an old woman!"

Wouldn't it be wonderful to be so accepting of one's appearance that we really could see and appreciate ourselves as others see and appreciate us? Not in some narcissistic fantasy of unblemished beauty, but see in ourselves a marvelous and interesting creature whose intrinsic worth is programmed within us at birth and grows ever finer and richer as we age. Perhaps this attitude is a gift of the spirit, a reflection of what it means to see one's body as a temple.

The challenge in our Western youth-oriented society is to stay visible as an older person, particularly an older person who is alone. When my widowed mother was living with me in her late eighties in Hawaii, I found it amusing that she would call one relative after another every weekend. This was before cell phones, and I'm sure that had she lived longer, she would have loved texting, emailing, and being on Facebook, for she was a social being who needed to be visible to others.

When we went out to eat, she would look around, see a couple she thought might be interesting, get up from our table and go start a conversation. This act embarrassed me as I thought it unseemly to intrude on strangers, but Mom had an unerring instinct for people. Her choices always seemed happy to talk to her and would often, on our way out, tell me what an interesting mother I had.

Still, my mother was lonely. I remember how shocked I was when she was landed in the hospital with an aneurysm that nearly cost her her life. Her doctor, who was my doctor, too, called me and asked me to pay more attention to her—not to her physical health, but to her need to feel that she mattered to someone. He had found her crying, inconsolably, as she lay in her hospital bed.

Mom lost her husband, my father, after 41 years of marriage—I was 40 at the time and knew nothing of the kind of grief that such major loss triggers. I had thought, after all the complaints she had about her marriage, and, in the end, how much of her energy and time was sapped by his lengthy illness, that being without him would be a relief. She still had my sisters and me to care about her, yet that attention wasn't enough.

After her recovery from that particular hospital stay, I began to accept her offers to wash dishes or make supper. Happily working in the kitchen, she'd collaborate with my husband Ted. Although he was a great cook, Ted would listen with interest to her and watch as she made her famous braised chuck steak with onions, stewed chicken with onions, and chicken soup with onions. The secret to her success, however, wasn't just onions; it was more in the way she hovered over the pan and the twist of the wrist as she turned browning meat or poultry. She shared her love by cooking and serving food, and in her old age, she found herself again standing at the stove.

Soon, I was the one who was isolated, which, in my busy life at the time, I appreciated. Mom, having regained a certain status, began to make bread and cinnamon rolls once more, which she shared with people at our church. Soon, she was being invited to go places with church members who found her stories fascinating.

I was working on a master's degree at the University of Hawaii where my mentor, a professor of psychology became interested in my mother and her stories. He invited her to lecture about her life in several of his classes. Mom thrived on this kind of attention. Her own mother died as she finished the fifth grade, and she was taken out of school and put to work, so she was deliriously happy to be accepted as a teacher late in life. Even her doctor made a video recording of her stories to use in teaching prospective doctors about the needs of older people. Of course, Mom was always a teacher; she just didn't know it until given her chance to shine.

In her 91st year before she left to visit my older sister in Delaware and, unexpectedly, to die there, she told me that being in Hawaii was the best time of her life. With a little help, she had found a way to become visible and important to others.

Many of us struggle to be seen when we are older. If we depend on children and grandchildren, we leave ourselves open to disappointment. It's not that our close relatives don't love us, but, like me, with my own mother, the thought that, in our aging, we might be lonely without a growing, active relationship or family of our own doesn't occur to them. Our children and our grandchildren are busy, still building their lives. We, who are older, are often left to simply reflect on our own lives. When we do converse with the younger generations, the conversation is invariably about them. Seldom do they want to know what motivates and interests us. Just as my mother's stories were to me, our life stories are old news to them.

The need for meaningful connection is basically unconscious when one is connected, intimately, with another human. One's companion is simply there; life is full and satisfying or full and not satisfying. The strength and importance of that connection was lost on me until I lost John. The loneliness I felt after John died was not just a condition of his absence. It was a pervasive feeling of being without substance.

As I began to rebuild my life, I felt less lonely, but never entirely free of the feeling that I might be invisible, that no one expected much from me anymore. With my increased involvement in church, twelve-step meetings and twelve-step work, friends, and writing, I became more visible to myself and stronger in resisting the temptation to give in to loneliness.

Like my mother, I find myself intruding on strangers, not to the extent of interrupting their dinners, but I do start conversations while waiting in line at the grocery store. Such idle talk provides a satisfying temporary antidote to loneliness and is also practice for taking larger risks, such as breaking into social conversations with my observations and opinions at parties or gatherings. I get rebuffed, occasionally, particularly if I politely challenge someone's certainty on a controversial subject. I may get a look of disbelief or a subtle dismissal with a change of subject, a signal that I'm in the wrong camp. With John by my side, such actions rarely occurred, and if they did, he was quick to rush to my defense. Without him, I'm learning to examine and refine my remarks along with the art of brushing off such snubs.

There are, however, those rare and beautiful moments when a kindred soul and I start talking and find not only common ground, but also pleasure in sharing our life stories with one another. Why don't I follow up on such encounters? With some people I have, but none have yet developed into close relationships.

What seems to work best is what my friend Ann in Seattle has done. Some years ago when she moved into a neighborhood, she began to go for morning coffee at a local shop. She soon joined a group that sat and talked about interesting subjects. Through the years the group has grown close, now celebrating one another's birthdays and having holiday celebrations together. What Ann likes best, beyond the stimulating conversation and laughter, is that people of all ages are attracted to their group and will join, briefly or permanently. Ann, who is older than I, finds herself a cherished and welcomed presence in a group of individuals intimately connected.

Healing a lonely heart takes time, effort, and faith in a positive outcome.

Chapter Twelve:
Embracing Age
(2010)

For most of us, the older we get, the more reluctant we become to celebrate birthdays unless we have one of those star celebration birthdays, the ones ending in zero or five with a big center-of-attention party. I love those parties. There's an element of triumph in them, a celebration of completing another ring on our personal tree of life, but then there is the aftermath, the "I can't believe" admission—I'm forty, fifty, sixty, sixty-five, and then, *seventy,* and, oh my God, am I really seventy-five with eighty lurking around the corner?

We hide from age. With all the new and improved hair dyes on the market, women, and increasingly men, cover up the gray and become, depending on their other skills in hiding wrinkles and settling flesh or lack of flesh on aging bones, ten or twenty years younger. With skillful cosmetic surgery and careful attention to diet, the possibility of being seen as a much younger person is within our grasp, if we have the fortune and fortitude such actions require. Some aging movie stars master this illusion so well that I question my own memory that asserts the star is older than I. I admit to a tiny bit of resentment when a star admits to being my age when I am sure she is older.

No one over thirty wants to be the oldest person in the room, with the exception, of course, of people like my mother who reveled in her old age. I think Mom never expected to live beyond sixty-five. When I was a youngster, she'd talk about being on the verge of death. Perhaps her insecurity about longevity was because she worked so hard. My sister and I were born to her when she was in her early forties. Just before my birth, my father moved her and my older half-sister from a city apartment in New Jersey to a country house in Maryland. That house, on riverfront property, which was the main attraction for my dad, was on the edge of nowhere. The river was hidden from sight by an acre or more of virgin weeds and brambles. The house itself was over a hundred years old and looked it. Mom said she could throw a pail of water on the wood floors in the living room, and it would disappear through the wide cracks in the floorboards before she even got a mop to it. It was in that same living room that I was born in a bed whose frame was "tied together with ropes." Mom was fond of telling this story and described the doctor as sweating in the August heat with my father slapping mosquitoes off his back. Water was pumped by hand, and for years the only light at night was from oil lamps, and, of course, there were either special chamber pots near the beds, which were freezing cold in winter, or the outhouse for personal needs. Yes, Mom, in tending her babies and working the scrub boards for the laundry, which she hauled outside to hang on those currently romantically-revered clotheslines, saw death as a release, I'm sure.

Once freed from the confines of her own home and hearth, and, living with me in Hawaii, Mom announced her age to anyone who'd listen. From her late eighties until she died at ninety-one, she wanted people to know she had made it. She walked the earth proudly as a person well into the big numbers.

Not so with most of us. When I was approaching 50, I felt appalled at becoming a half-century old. A very good friend was only a year behind me, and I took comfort in that fact, for she looked good and acted as a role model for me. Then she found her true birth certificate. Her mother had convinced her when she was young and pregnant by her boyfriend that she was sixteen and could be married; only she wasn't sixteen. She was two years younger, which with us both approaching fifty, made her, at least, three years younger than I! This startling news was exhilarating for her, but for me, it was a bruising blow to the way I saw myself. I wasn't prepared to march into the second half of my life's century (God willing) without the accompaniment of my friend. Worse, I was angrily and unreasonably jealous of her, as if she had deliberately misrepresented herself to gain the glory of suddenly losing a couple of years of aging. What nonsense! Yet, in that time of life being as young as my friend, and not a whole span of three years older, was *so* important.

Perhaps the desire to be young, fit, and attractive is biologically set in us. We are, after all, creatures of the earth designed to fulfill a responsibility to reproduce our kind. We need to be young and attractive to mates to implant and birth babies. We view the heady times of our youth as some of the most desirable years of our lives, so we, naturally, want to cling to the illusion of still being so vital that we need never consider an end to life. The will to live is so strong that living itself, to most of us, implies being strong and healthy as well, unencumbered by the ills of aging.

Birthdays are a nasty reminder that the years are adding up. We are finite creatures, unable to extend our lifetimes much beyond an average age, which in itself varies greatly in the world (39.5 years in Swaziland to 81 years in Japan). My personal goal is 100 years, but even then, setting a goal admits to an ending. It is easier, perhaps even healthier, to live with a certain amount of denial about death, at least up to the time when we have to think of our own ending.

No wonder we dye our hair and look for signs of youth in ourselves and others!

There comes a time, though, when being young when we are old, is ridiculous. Our church family made a project out of repairing trails at a youth retreat in the Santa Cruz Mountains of California. I went along, fully intending to climb the rough trails and do my part, despite being 74 at the time and having breathing problems from smoking cigarettes during my invincible, youthful years. I gamely started out with the others, among them a two-year-old who scrambled easily up the trail, but as the terrain became steep and littered with fallen trees alongside crumbling cliff sides, I faltered. No way could I lift my oxygen-hungry legs over the next fallen tree. My lungs screamed for me to stop. I was forced to admit that I couldn't keep up with my younger companions; indeed, I was a liability to them, as they had had to stop often to help me. I gave up, and returned by myself to camp.

Once rested, I began to gather supplies, wash lettuce, slice tomatoes, arrange cold cuts on platters, look for drinks, stock up on ice, and in general, get the camp ready for lunch. When the trail workers returned, there was much gratitude that lunch was ready for them, and so, in this different role, I made my life useful in a way appropriate to my age.

It was a significant moment for me, though, for I had fully expected to be out on the trail with the rest of the group. Somehow I had seen myself as vigorous as they; that observation just wasn't accurate. There are people my age who are in good physical shape and, unhampered by bodily limitations, are able to keep up with younger people. Walking back down that trail with the taste of defeat and disappointment in my mouth was hard. I wanted to cry. Instead, I stopped by the camp's fire pit, sat on a bench there and looked up at the magnificent redwoods providing their cover of age and comfort to me. I wondered if the patient trees ever felt old and useless. The thought made me laugh. Attributing negative human qualities to trees who simply have a place in the world and serve their purpose where planted was a ludicrous notion. Yet, the lesson of serving where planted stuck. That was when I decided to make lunch.

I accepted I was a woman of a certain age that day, but I didn't accept that, being a woman of a certain age made me weak and helpless. I looked for tasks I could do, and let go of the ones I knew I couldn't.

My acceptance brought me a certain status. After lunch, middle-aged members of our group decided to climb an easier trail, and I asked to go along. As we walked, someone handed me his walking stick, and I found myself walking more easily up steep terrain. When I had to stop to catch my breath, everyone stopped, and we took the time to marvel at the joys of nature all around us. Getting to our destination involved getting over some fallen trees and navigating slippery and hazardous slopes. It was suggested I stay back and wait for the walkers to complete the trip and come back down for me. I didn't stay back. With the patient concern of my comrades, their helping hands, and the stick, I was able to get within sight of the final destination, a cave in the face of a cliff, half-hidden behind a narrow ledge of overgrown trail. Someone had placed a bench a short distance from the trail to the cave, and it was there I planted myself to watch my comrades finish the walk. A couple stayed behind with me, giving me company and a wise example of enacting choice in their own decision not to complete the walk. Their choice had nothing to do with limitation, but everything to do with courtesy, respect and friendship for me.

I learned that day that accepting my age and limitations gave others the opportunity to serve me and to feel useful in that service. We became, in essence, gifts to one another.

In any age, we isolate ourselves by not accepting who we are. In our busy world we often forget that we are, indeed, people, not our roles. Yet that position of roles is how we organize life. In the beginning we are babies, toddlers, school children, adolescents and young adults, living up to the expectations of each stage whether we want to or not. There is little time for reflection as we do the tasks of growing up. Once grown, we lose ourselves in jobs or careers and take on partners and raise families. Somewhere along the line we are asked to take care of others, aged parents or other relatives or, altruistically, anyone who needs our help. As we approach old age, losses begin to overwhelm us. We have lived competently for such a long time that we resent the aches and pains that move in on us. We reject, as long as we can, the ugly, but sturdy, shoes that keep us from falling or, when shoes are not enough, we push against buying that first cane or, God forbid, the walker. As much as old age makes us invisible as persons, in a cruel irony, old age makes visible the handicaps and vicissitudes that bedevil us. Our first reaction is to be angry. We feel betrayed by our bodies.

When our minds began to cloud, or the words, we once so easily rolled off our tongues, begin to lock themselves in impossible areas of our minds, we feel frightened. To give into this fear, to feel it and talk about it makes the condition all too real. We leap to disastrous conclusions, so most of us hide our verbal handicaps as long we can. My favorite trick is to say that I'm grateful I have such a large and sophisticated brain that I can afford to lose a few brain cells here and there. But, secretly, wouldn't it be beyond awful to get Alzheimer's?

People do get Alzheimer's or dementia of various sorts and degrees, and, somehow, they and their families learn to live with these afflictions. There is even a kind of grace in it all as evidenced by those who have written stories about these diseases in their loved ones.

Coping with the imagined disease, the one we are sure we are heading toward by the symptoms cropping up in us, is worse, in a way, because we still have hope that these disasters will not befall us. Our task is to learn to cope with our fears, to quiet our anxieties and, as always, come back to the moment in which we are living in a relatively able state.

The secret to aging is embracing age as it occurs in us. When I walked the cobblestone streets of Europe on my cruise and tour of the Mediterranean, I used John's cane. I could have walked without it, but I used it because I didn't want to break a leg or arm in a fall and ruin my travels. Twenty years earlier, walking some of the same streets with John and my son Steve, I walked with the confidence of a relatively young middle-aged body, not even thinking about a fall, let alone a cane.

Like most of life, being an older person requires adjustments not only in what and how we do our lives, but in our attitudes as well. I can see life at 75 as a burden, or I can see it as a challenge. I choose to challenge myself. I am not an ex-president, who in his eighties, jumps out of an airplane to celebrate his birthdays, yet I am ready and willing to see if there are activities I *can* tackle. I am not so much afraid of failure anymore. It's not that I have to prove myself to myself or prove myself to others; it's a matter of keeping active, staying alive and alert as long as I can.

At 80 Clint Eastwood still makes significant movies and shows no signs of stopping. In a 2010 magazine article, he talks of challenging himself with tasks that tax his brain and force him to think. He seems always ready to learn something new. I'd say that Clint Eastwood is living his old age, buoyed by his positive attitude, and is successful because he doesn't seem to be afraid of failure, either.

The gift of old age is to be able to see ourselves as we are. If we dare to acknowledge that we have limitations along with our talents, we find that we are genuine beings, capable of moving behind our limitations by graciously accepting and using the talents we were given.

My friends live lives that are different than mine, but equally as fulfilling. Some of them have become resources to their children who are balancing jobs and growing families. These adult children depend on their mothers and fathers to pick up grandchildren after school, ferry the kids to their meetings or after-school activities, and cook a meal or two, or to be there in an emergency. My friends don't live in rocking chairs with shawls over their shoulders, waiting for the next visit from family. They are happily useful.

Conversely, we are old enough *not* to do what we don't want to do. If we are lucky, by the time we have begun to feel our age, we have learned to say *no* to tasks that aren't fulfilling and *yes* to ones that give our lives meaning. For instance, I treat myself to house cleaners twice a month because I have learned to choose to devote my energy to the fulfilling task of writing. I don't need to be an unwilling martyr to house cleaning. Conversely, women, who love house cleaning or gardening or volunteering, might be appalled if asked to write stories about their lives. We can and do respect one another's choices as we age for we are no longer competing for attention; we are acting in our own best interest by making fulfilling choices.

Being old provides opportunity to live freely. So, if we want to, we can reach for our hair dyes, because dyeing gray hair is a choice. We are no longer hiding our age, we are accenting our choice to be a redhead or a blonde or a brunette. If our hair thins, then colored strands may make more sense to us than straggly locks of gray. On the other hand, beautiful heads of white or gray show up in old age, and keeping that natural look is also a choice. We live out the freedom of our aging selves.

Chapter Thirteen:
Forgotten Memories
(2006–2010)

After losing John, I must have drunk from the waters of Lethe, that mythical river of Hades that allows one to forget everything. Certainly the hard facts of living with him during the last years of his life were all but forgotten as I continued to write this book and started to enjoy the new life I was fashioning for myself.

Then one day, in looking for paper to write a quick note to myself, I dipped a hand into a file folder where I sometimes put scrap paper. Out came a copy of an early 2007 email I had written to my sisters, filled with vivid details of John's sufferings and my own grueling efforts to take care of him. As I reread the email, the memory of my last years with John came crashing in on me, leaving me breathless and disturbed.

When John and I begin living together, I had had some awareness that I'd probably have to care for him in his last days, since he was much older than I. Mine was a naive and romantic notion of gracefully supporting him through a brief and reasonably painless illness. The reality was stark and unrelenting, a challenge that sorely tested my physical and emotional limits.

Our problems begin in earnest when John had what he referred to as his own September 11th incident in 2006. On that day, we were parked in the lot in front of his podiatrist's office. I asked John to stay in the car while I took his walker out of the trunk. Being stubbornly independent, he ignored me and got out of the car, leaning his backside on the front fender. I watched him take out his handkerchief to blow his nose and then, in a surreal slow-motion movement, he keeled over in a strangely elegant, eerily quiet, straight-line fall, landing nose first on the hard blacktop pavement.

"John!" I screamed. There was no answer—just stillness. He lay face down in a fast-forming pool of blood. *He's dead,* I thought, *he's dead!* I knelt beside him, calling his name, "John. John. Are you okay?"

Of course, he wasn't okay, but I wanted to hear him say something, anything to let me know he was alive. Another patient called to me from the door of the office, "I told them inside. An ambulance is coming."

John moaned. "My neck," he said, "my neck. Get me up."

Among his many ills, John suffered from spinal stenosis with a stiff and aching neck. He couldn't lie comfortably on his stomach.

"No, John, stay down," I begged. The podiatrist came from his office with a blanket. We dared not lift John's head. When the ambulance came, the attendants found him bruised and battered, but with nothing broken, except the skin on his forehead. Later, in the hospital, he was taken to surgery to bind his fragile forehead skin with surgical glue. Because of his age, 94 at the time, and the trauma of the fall and the surgery, he was admitted.

I felt scared and angry. I immediately repressed these unwanted feelings as selfishness. It wasn't about me; John was the one who was hurt. Never mind that I was overloaded with the work of running the household and managing John's needs all on my own! Still, this full-time job with no pay or benefits required rules and boundaries to work. Why couldn't John have listened to me and stayed in the car until I could see him safely connected with his walker? I felt guilty for even entertaining these thoughts. After all, John hadn't meant to fall. His desire for some degree of independent action was understandable. In my concern for his safety, I had turned into a nag, and I hated that role. Now, I was blaming myself.

Yes, I loved John. I loved him enough to continue to try to give him some semblance of a normal life at home while losing my own independence and freedom. I loved him enough to be a martyr while despising the necessity for recognizing this feeling. Paramount to my anger was my helplessness. With all my intelligence and education, I was powerless over the relentless decline of John's body and health; I couldn't fix him. I couldn't stop the inexorable decline. All I could do was to be there for him and care for him despite my own frustrations, limitations and fears.

After a few days, John was transferred from acute care to the hospital's rehabilitation facility where I went to visit daily and participate with him in his physical and occupational therapy. My part was to be officially trained as his caregiver. Years before I had done similar training with him after he underwent a procedure for treatment of his neck issues. Now, I learned, once more, how to assist him in getting in and out of the car, how to help direct him to his feet when he fell, and how to help him do his balance exercises. He was home after eleven days of inpatient treatment.

During his time in rehab, John's family came from Colorado, Grass Valley, and Santa Cruz, California and my son and his partner from San Jose. We had a party in the rehab recreation room. The injured head of the family with his stitched forehead, his black eyes, and his swollen face held court amidst pizza boxes, a couple of bottles of surreptitious wine for those who wanted it, and some flavored tea drink and water for the rest of us. It was there, to the delight of Sean, his teenaged grandson, that John convinced his son Michael to buy a car for Sean. He teased and cajoled and reminded Michael of the drama he had planned in presenting him with his first car, an MG convertible. The MG was parked on the street when John and Michael walked up to admire it. "Get in," John said. "See how it feels." Michael was shocked. "We can't do that, Dad. This is somebody's car!"

"Oh, go ahead. He won't mind," John insisted and when Michael obeyed, John reached in his pocket and handed his son the keys. Months after this remembrance, when Michael gave Sean his own car, he pulled nearly the same trick as his father, this time the story being that the used red BMW Sean had his heart set on was sold to someone else. A thoroughly disappointed Sean drove the family car home from the dealer's to find his dream car parked in the driveway.

The family party in rehab that day was an interlude of joy in the gathering storm of grief to come.

Once home, Medicare provided a power wheelchair for John. Later we purchased an electric scooter. The wheelchair was awkward for John to operate and soon the walls of the house were gouged and scarred as well as the dining room table, which he ran into regularly at mealtimes.

"John, please," I'd shout over the agonizing screech of the chair as it strained against and finally pushed a resistant and heavy oak dining room table precariously close to glass sliding doors a few short feet away. "Turn it off! Turn it off!" My heart calmed when he managed to reverse the chair's direction, freeing the badly gouged table. At least, the sliding doors stayed intact.

John preferred to use his walker in the house, but the walker didn't always work for him. He began falling again; One week, he fell three days in a row.

Besides the falls, John had facial nerve pain from surgery for a dry socket that occurred after he had the rest of his teeth extracted in May 2006. In that year, John was treated by two different dentists, had two sets of dentures made, refused to consistently wear either because of his pain, lost weight when he couldn't comfortably eat, and finally, after 31 dental visits, sought relief from his primary doctor. His doctor prescribed Tegretol on top of all the other meds John took.

The day the doctor prescribed the new medication and before he took it, John came into the house, was hurrying to the bathroom with his walker and fell against the glass doors of the TV console. One door of the tempered glass shattered. I came running when I heard the crash. A large patch of his skin beneath one arm was hanging loosely. I was horrified but I reacted immediately, wriggling myself between his back and the console to prevent further injury from the glass. I tried to get him up.

He wouldn't let me call 911, so we scooted away from the glass, over to my hassock where I left him leaning and resting on the hassock, but sitting on the floor while I brought over his electric wheelchair. He managed to get up enough for me to push him into the wheelchair. Not trusting his driving, I guided the wheelchair to the bathroom, bandaged John's wounds, and then maneuvered us back to the living room where I cleaned up glass in and around the console, in the VCR, the tapes, and in the DVD player.

That night I gave him his first Tegretol. It worked. Without the pain he enjoyed eating a meal. Then he sat down to watch TV with me. It soon became apparent that he couldn't track the stories. When he became agitated, I turned off the TV and we went to bed.

On Sunday, he seemed agitated again. "This coffee's not hot."

"Where's the newspaper?"

"Can you get me a nail file?" He was increasingly dissatisfied, running me ragged with small errands. If I left the room to use the computer, he would get up to go to the bathroom without me, determined to prove he could walk unassisted. On one such secret trip to the bathroom, I heard him fall. This time he fell between his recliner and his chair. Again, he wouldn't let me call 911 and we struggled together to get him back into his recliner. He didn't want to go see his doctor. Falls were so common with him that there seemed to be a degree of acceptance in him that he would fall. It became my job to judge whether he needed a doctor. On this occasion, I judged wrong, but I was so exhausted that I just wanted to sit down myself, but I couldn't. There was more to do.

I fed John, gave him his medication, cleaned up, and finally sat down to watch TV with him. He was watching, but not reacting to the shows. Finally, he admitted his helplessness, "I can't tell what is happening anymore," he said in a low voice, barely concealing fear.

"It's okay. You're tired." I made this reasonable excuse for him to not lose hope. "Let's go to bed."

That night he woke me five times to go to the bathroom. I had to get up with him and assist him because his legs were rubbery, and I knew he would fall. Every time I tried to go back to sleep, I was anxious, thinking about what would happen if he got up by himself and fell again. *Damn it!* I needed to sleep. *Just, please, let me sleep.*

John woke me from a fitful sleep at 6:30 in the morning. "Take me to the hospital," he said. I was groggy and exhausted. I wanted everything to stop, simply stop. "I have a pain in my chest," he said.

"Where?" I asked, wearily, barely lifting my head from the pillow. He indicated his ribs on the right side. I didn't look at his side. I looked at his face. His face told me he was fine, good color, no gray. I looked to see whether he was sweating—no, he wasn't—and then I asked if he had pain anywhere else. No, he didn't. There was no arm or shoulder pain. At this point, I made the judgment that he wasn't having a heart attack. I was too tired for a heart attack, too physically and emotionally drained to take in any more problems. I put my head on my pillow and surrendered. If I was wrong, I was ready for a heart attack to come end it all for him and even for me.

Although I didn't sleep, I waited until just before the doctor's office opened at nine to get him up and dressed. I called his doctor who said to take him to the emergency room where he was diagnosed with a broken rib. It was there I finally looked at his side and noticed the tremendously large bruise over the broken rib that had been the source of his chest pain.

The emergency doctors sent him home. By the time I got him settled in his power chair, it was two o'clock in the afternoon. Besides not having any sleep and taking responsibility for the emergency, I had not eaten breakfast, although I had managed to give John some. I had not eaten lunch, nor had he. He wanted sherry instead of lunch. His doctor had told him he could have one glass of wine with dinner. It wasn't dinnertime, and I was in no mood to give him sherry and make him even more vulnerable to falling.

"You can't have sherry," I said.

"I'll get it myself," he answered emphatically, driving his wheelchair to the pantry.

I went a little crazy. "No, you don't," I said, snatching the bottle out of the cupboard and taking it to the sink. I poured the contents down the drain and turned to put the bottle in the recycling can. John came at me with the wheelchair.

I reached for the controls and turned him around and drove him, in the chair, to the dining table. I intended to feed him; then reality hit me. *This is nuts! This is crazy.* I picked up the phone and called our caregiver Heidi, even though John resented giving up the $12 an hour we paid her.

When she arrived, I felt as if an angel had come from heaven. She was calm and calmed us both. I was able to feed myself and John while Heidi did dishes, tidied up the house, started the laundry, and made the bed. I asked her to stay while I got some sleep. At five o'clock, I woke with the wheelchair in the bedroom. John wanted to go to the bathroom. Heidi apologized, but said John insisted I'd had enough sleep! So Heidi went home, and I went back to work.

On Tuesday, Heidi came and sat with John while I went to a twelve-step meeting. After the meeting, since I was in my now normal tired state, a friend drove me in my car to the hearing aid center to get John's hearing aids cleaned; he had complained he couldn't hear. The same friend also came on Wednesday to stay with John so I could go to my women's meeting and out to lunch with them. I felt as if I were a thief, snatching time for myself, time away from relentless duties, time for a brief enjoyment of my own, time to remember how to breathe myself.

On Wednesday night, John was really out of it. He didn't know who I was. He was confused on Sunday night as well, asking me who else was in the house—there was no one else—and whether they were going to stay overnight. At least on Sunday he knew who I was. Heidi told me that on Tuesday he had said to her he had been to "Snowflake," meaning the emergency room. When he didn't know me on Wednesday, I was upset. The John I knew and loved was rapidly leaving, slipping away into a land where I didn't exist for him. The sudden flood of searing pain, of grief raw and unbidden, was unbearable. I swallowed hard to control it. I couldn't give in. Not yet.

I called the doctor on Thursday. Wondering whether it might be Alzheimer's, he decided I should stop all medication that might be altering John's mental state. The Tegretol was the first to go. The Luvox, Efforex, and Requip were to be stopped after we saw what happened after discontinuing Tegretol. I hoped John wouldn't have a severe reaction.

The doctor said that if we are "crashing and burning" like we had been doing, to take John to the emergency room where he'd arrange an overnight stay to do a brain scan and some other tests. Then he would transfer him to a skilled nursing facility, which Medicare would initially pay for. We would talk after that, he said, implying, but not actually saying, custodial care. In the meantime, the doctor's nurse would work on a plan to get Home Health Care help for us. Finally, we qualified for some help!

A friend came by with lunch, then did the dishes for me, folded laundry, made our bed, and sat and read while John and I napped. Thank God for friends.

About six o'clock that night John tried to go to the bathroom again with his walker. He made a turn and fell in the hallway. He wanted me to help him up and I tried, but it was too hard. I had no strength left in my arms. My right thumb was hurting (it was later diagnosed as severely strained.)

"I'm going to call 911," I said, reaching for the phone.

"No, don't," John pleaded. "Just give me your hand."

"I can't, John. I can't pick you up. Let me call 911."

"No. No 911." He squirmed, trying to get his feet under him. He couldn't. I looked at him and my heart broke, but I had no more strength, nothing more to give.

"Pick yourself up then," I said. He struggled. I bit my lips to hold back tears as I watched him, but I didn't offer my hand. I felt so guilty. What a bad person I was to watch him suffering so without doing anything for him!

John sighed, "Call 911," he said. Three strong paramedic/firemen came, picked him up easily, and settled him in his recliner. It was wonderful, and there was no charge for the service.

John was okay. When we went to bed, I put double paper pads on him and asked him to stay in bed all night. He said he would, and he did; I slept soundly. In the morning he awoke, my old John again; he knew me and was glad to be with me. The confusion was gone. It was the Tegretol, after all, that triggered the mental state that mirrored Alzheimer's, not full-blown dementia. My relief was immense.

Our difficulties did not end there, however. I had gallstones and scheduled an operation in May. I needed a place for John to stay temporarily.

Placing a loved one in a nursing facility is very difficult. John never wanted to go into custodial care, but agreed to go for a week while I had my gall bladder removed. I found a place I thought suitable. We had to pay $100 a day out of pocket, since Medicare doesn't cover such stays, but that cost was cheaper than twenty-four hour at-home care, which ran from $15 to $22 an hour at that time.

He hated it. His roommate slept all day and went to bed after supper, complaining if John came into the room and turned on the light. John sat in a wheelchair in the hall, calling me on his cell phone. "Take me home, please," he begged.

"I can't John. I just got home from the hospital. I need to rest. I can't take care of you. Please stay just a little while."

"It's purgatory here," he complained. "No one talks to me." Indeed many of the residents were cognitively impaired, living in their own unknown worlds, doing daily routines of eating, being bathed and medicated, and sleeping. I hadn't seen that dimension in the home the day I first checked out the place, for I had arrived during a happy time of recreation with a piano being played and some residents playing board games in the dining room. The residents, sitting in a circle of wheelchairs in the living room and listening to the piano concert, seemed serene. The place smelled clean, no strong odor of disinfectant covering up any unpleasant odor.

"I'm sorry, John. It's only a little while. I'll take you home in a few days."

In those few days, John fell twice, the first time the day after my surgery, the second, two days after that. The facility told me after the first fall that he had bruised his arm. In a telephone call, I reiterated to the director that her attendants needed to watch John carefully, as his doctor had written on the order for his care that he was at high risk for falls.

Nevertheless he fell a second time, broke his nose, had to have stitches in his forehead, and suffered numerous abrasions on his arms and hands. Twice, I had to interrupt my recovery from surgery to go and see John, once for his arm injury, the second time to take him to his own doctor who told me John had also torn the rotator cuff in his right shoulder in his second fall.

I felt terrible. My surgery, thankfully, was done in a laparoscopic procedure, so there was no major incision to heal. I was able to stay home alone, planning to rest and recover for a week. Although the surgery was necessary for me to regain my energy and health to take care of John, I felt agonizing guilt for having the surgery and leaving him in a facility that, with his falls and injuries, caused him so much pain. His shoulder pain never ceased after that.

I reported the facility to the state licensing office, but had neither the heart nor the energy to do more than that.

I hoped my complaint would result in changes in the facility or, at least, be part of the record so others could be wary of care at that facility.

The family was appalled at our situation. Charmaine, John's daughter-in-law, flew in from Denver to help us through my first week home with John. We also had Heidi, our part-time caregiver, helping us, but no matter who was here, John called on me first when he wanted help of any kind.

John never wanted to be put into a nursing home again, and I promised him that I would not do so, unless it was absolutely necessary. It was obvious, though, that he was becoming frailer and that, if he didn't die, I would have to consider a nursing facility for him. We talked about the cost, which led us to seek the advice of an attorney, an elder advocate, who told us what to expect. Because we weren't married in the eyes of the federal government, since domestic partnerships were recognized only by states in which they were legal, my assets weren't in jeopardy, but John's were. The attorney showed us how to protect John's assets by transferring them, legally, to me. Later, after John died, I was able to give his children and grandchildren their inheritances because of this action and keep the portion John left to me.

Growing older myself, with my companion in failing health, and yet trying to cope with all the ordinary and extraordinary tasks, emergency situations, and medical and legal decisions to be made was overwhelming. I was grateful that I had resources and friends and family to help, but I was also angry and frustrated that there had been no way of knowing and preparing myself for the hardest physical and emotional labor I have ever done, and the suffering I experienced. Gail Sheehy had yet to publish her excellent book, *Passages in Caregiving: Turning Chaos into Confidence*, which I surely could have used.

I am not alone. Many seniors face difficult choices when unable to care for loved ones at home. Because Medicare won't pay for custodial care in nursing homes, seniors have to spend down their assets before being considered for Medicaid, a program that pays for such care if one is poor. If married, the "community" spouse (the one who resides at home) is allowed the home and just half of the couple's savings, a drastic cut for most people. Some seniors divorce to protect assets, a painful action that nevertheless allows the "community" spouse to continue to live with some sense of security. John was never on the Medicaid program, though we were headed in that direction when he died. He never opted for long-term care insurance because of its costs and an uncertain understanding of just what is covered.

In that awful year of so much pain for both John and me, there were a couple of trips I took. One was to Maryland to join in the celebration of my college roommate's 50th wedding anniversary and then to spend a week in Delaware visiting with my sisters. I took a second trip in September, a tour of Canada's eastern cities and Niagara Falls, a place I wanted to see before I died. My death seemed a possibility, as people warned me that caregivers often die before their sick spouses do. To give me that travel time and the peace of mind that John was being taken care of properly, John's daughter Cathy and his daughter-in-law Charmaine came to stay with him, using Heidi to aid them. It was the best of worlds for Cathy and Charmaine, who related to one another like beloved sisters, and for John, who, although he missed me and had to speak to me every day by phone, enjoyed the security of having his family with him. He didn't fall.

The magnificent Niagara Falls felt like a blessing. I stood, with many others clad in useless blue plastic rain sheaths in the bow of the Maid of the Mist tour boat, and got happily soaked. I actually allowed the water of the mist, kicked up by the powerful falls, to pass my lips as if I were drinking in a potent formula for renewed life. I thought of my mother, who had felt the same way about Niagara Falls; I was grateful to be there. Later, on the path above the falls, I watched the amazing river water calmly approach its edge and obediently spill over. I was standing by a woman who identified herself as a retired nun. Mesmerized by the wonder before us, we spontaneously broke into song, "How great Thou art. How great Thou art."

Once home, I scheduled another surgery. This time it was a hammertoe that needed attention. The surgery was minor, and I healed quickly. A specialist finally examined my thumb and a brace was made to use until it healed. It seemed as if all my health problems were popping up in concert with taking care of John. Meanwhile, John was convinced there was something additionally wrong with him. He asked his doctor for a colonoscopy and we found a gastroenterologist that determined he could do a virtual colonoscopy on John.

We started the preparation on a Tuesday. The process involves a liquid diet of limited food choices and taking very strong laxatives, all calculated to completely clean the bowel before the procedure. John had always disliked drinking water and found swallowing difficult. His body was probably breaking down even then, but I didn't recognize the process. His doctor never said to me that John was dying; on the contrary, he was encouraging us to believe John would make it to his 100th birthday. I realize, now, that many doctors are reluctant to face death in a patient, for all their training has conditioned them to believe in their abilities to heal. This was so with John's doctor.

It was tortuous to watch John struggle to drink quart after quart of water with the prescribed preparation in it.

After two days of the procedure, John was so weak that he couldn't stand. "I'm cold," he said at ten o'clock that night, and indeed he was shivering. I piled woolen blankets on him as he sat in his recliner, but still he shivered. I asked him to get up. He couldn't stand. I wrestled him onto the seat of his walker and pushed him into the bedroom and then had to wrestle him onto the bed. I felt like crying, but there was no time for tears. He was hardly able to cooperate and flopped around like a caught fish, so I piled the covers and blankets on him and raced to the phone to call the doctor. His gastroenterologist was not on duty, and I didn't receive a call back. When I got back to the bedroom, John seemed better, and I crawled, exhausted again, into bed beside him. I hardly closed my eyes before he started to vomit all the volumes of watery liquid he had consumed.

I jumped from the bed and tried to get him up out of the mess, but only managed to pull off his nightshirt. He still was limp in his movements and unable to follow instructions. I called 911. The paramedics came. Even they had trouble getting him on a stretcher to carry him out to the ambulance waiting to take him to the hospital.

He was diagnosed with bronchitis and pneumonia. The shivering was from a fever. The diarrhea, of course, was from the bowel prep. After a few days in the hospital, he was better.

John never came home after that. Nor did he have the colonoscopy. He went from one skilled nursing facility near our home that didn't accept Medicaid to another, which, was to be his home for the rest of his life. I just couldn't take care of him anymore. Once his Medicare rehab nursing benefits ran out, he would be eligible for Medicaid funds.

It was heartbreaking to watch him struggle with physical therapy tasks he no longer had strength to perform, but which had to be done to satisfy Medicare payment requirements. Two days before he died, I came upon him and his therapist walking the parallel bars in the therapy room. John was lying, limply, on her shoulder, eyes closed wearily, as she walked with him. "Stop it," I ordered, tears in my eyes. "Can't you see he can't walk?"

The therapist immediately put him in his wheelchair where John revived. She gave him a balloon to bat to me as I stood before him. We were smiling at one another, slowly and tenderly batting the balloon, back and forth, back and forth, between us. In a strange way it felt like dancing, an activity we had especially loved to do together. What s sweet moment for me to store and treasure. It reminded me of earlier times, dancing with his walker between us, happy to be together, no matter what.

John called his former brother-in-law from the nursing home, "Can you believe this, Joe? That I'm ending up here?" He didn't want to be in that nursing home, nor any other, and we talked nearly every day about this issue. Always, he reiterated that he *would* stay because it was best for me to have him cared for there. It was best for him as well, but I never stressed that because it was important for John to feel he was doing something for me. Near the end, he began to get to know and appreciate the nurses and aides who took care of him. He was in custodial care for a little over two months before he died.

A friend asked me, recently, if I regretted putting John in the nursing home. If I had known he was dying, that he would die so quickly after being put in custodial care, I would have overridden his objection to spending money on twenty-four-hour care and would have hired help to keep him home. Home is the best place to die; yet, at the point I made the choice to put him into custodial care, I couldn't foresee the future. I just knew what we were doing didn't work anymore. The nursing home I chose was a good one for John and for me; so, no, I don't regret placing him there. Reliving the relentless and painful moments of that last year leads me back to seek the blessed forgetfulness of Lethe once more. Even two and half years later, my body tenses when I visit those memories. Perhaps there will be a time when sweet lethargy visits, maybe, on a lazy day on a beach in Hawaii.

Chapter Fourteen:
Caroling
(2009)

When I decided to go Christmas caroling with some members of our church, I expected the Hallmark card version of singing in the streets to happy families standing in the doorway of a well-lighted home, perhaps with the aroma of Christmas cookies baking and hot chocolate brewing, an anticipated award for our labors, but the plan wasn't to sing to our immediate neighbors or even to walk for that matter.

In the church parking lot stood Rosie the Trolley, an old fashioned red trolley car with wood and brass interiors, rented from the city of Santa Rosa for this occasion. The trolley was festively decorated with red and green Christmas hangings. When I arrived, Rosie was full of choir members, children, and other congregants, who, as I, liked to sing, especially the old Christmas carols. Popcorn and a variety of cookies were being consumed. Those who had brought goodies shared them. The excited chatter of the children reminded me of my own childhood elation at being included in an important adult activity.

As we chugged out of the parking lot, we began to hum; our musical tone underlined the deep-throated noise of gears being shifted, but soon our hums gave way to a glorious proclamation: "Joy to the world, the Lord is come." Our voices harmonized and blended, filling the trolley with glowing warmth, stoking my spirit and giving me a sense of transcendence.

The children sang as loudly and enthusiastically as the adults as we wended our way toward our destination, Bethlehem Towers, a senior living residence downtown. Once inside, I was disappointed that there were few residents in the large living room off the lobby, but there was a piano. Our choir director handed out music sheets of a Christmas song I didn't know.

"I can't sing this." I said.

"Sure you can," she countered. "You heard us sing it last Sunday." She thrust the sheets in my hand and moved on. Our pianist began to play and choir members began to sing, and so did I, just as if I had known the song all my life. Wonderful what a little encouragement can do for one's confidence! Of course, there were parts where I was behind, but I either caught up or jumped to the part that the others were singing. It didn't matter. Our scant audience appreciated our effort. When we left, I wondered just how successful our caroling would be that evening. Would we indeed be singing for others as well as ourselves?

Our next destination was a nursing home. My heart sank a little when I realized we were going to sing in nursing homes. I hoped we would not go to the one where John had died since in three days the second anniversary of his death would make its mark. There were so many reminders of John and his last days. Would I ever get used to reliving sadness when driving past the hospital where he spent so much time, or the facility at Spring Lake Village where he was in rehab, or even the funeral home where we said the last goodbye? When would these buildings become ordinary again?

As we walked into the Golden Living Center, a place my son Steve and I had looked at for John but rejected, I was surprised at the feeling of peace that came over me. What a different perspective I could have with no one I knew and loved living there! Somewhere down the hall, a guitar was playing and people were already singing "Jingle Bells." We stood in the hallway, some of us able to fit into the doorway of the recreation room where people were singing. We sang along, bringing our vocal swell and harmonies to the jaunty tune. When "Jingle Bells" came to an end, we were invited in, and I saw our audience, elders in wheelchairs, looking alert, clean and satisfied. Many smiled as we sang more songs with them. Admittedly, these were residents willing and able to leave their rooms for this event, and so were motivated toward enjoyment, but their attentive presence gave me pause.

Now, that I wasn't personally involved with John as a patient, I began to think of how it must be to spend your last years in such a place. All your physical needs are met—maybe not in the timely fashion they would be met by caregivers in your own home—but met. If you are lucky, family comes to visit. There are daily activities planned that provide some stimulation and meaning in life. Being in a secure place is a primary advantage of living in a nursing facility. I remember John expressing that security even as he told me he wanted to go home.

How would I fare if I were sitting there in a wheelchair, listening to music provided by a neighborhood church? I don't know, but I think that once I had accepted the necessity for living there, I might do quite well if I weren't totally incapacitated. I imagine myself making a life, talking to people, encouraging them when they feel depressed, talking to staff, asking about their home lives, getting to know who is taking care of me and making friends. If I still had some skills left, I might ask to lead a discussion group. My son would visit and take me out once in awhile to see what the outside world was doing. And, yes, I, too, would want to go home, home to a life that I knew was over, would never again be re-created even in the finest nursing home. It would be at this point that I'd realize that, once again, I was rebuilding my life.

Perhaps that rebuilding of life, even as one moves toward the end of life, is what I sensed in the seniors in that nursing home recreation room. These seniors in wheelchairs were accepting life on life's terms, finding appreciation for what they were experiencing, and even enjoyment in the opportunities offered them.

What would such a place be like if I had dementia? What would I know and what wouldn't I know? How would I communicate?

Pat, my friend with dementia, is my teacher in this instance. Her care home is small with seven women in residence. A young woman owns the place and keeps everything and everyone scrupulously clean. On my last visit, I was with Pat's daughter Donna.

We woke Pat when we came into her room. She looked at me, briefly, and then her face lit up; before her illness, she'd greet me, joyfully; I was her best friend. I had no idea whether or not she really knew me now. I felt she did, but Donna seemed to think that she recognizes no one. "My mother is a good actress," she told me.

Was Pat acting? It seems to me that if a person makes a choice to act as if she knows me, that there is some sort of conscious knowing there. Pat spoke, but her words were garbled sounds. The cadence was there, as if her brain were truly processing thought and making sounds to communicate that thought.

Would I, if stricken by dementia, feel as if I were locked into my own inner world, unable to present an intelligible self to others? Pat's smile and the pleasure that registered on her face made me think that there was still joy in her life, a joy connected with seeing people she loved whether she was able to identify us or not. Would I be blessed with such grace?

When we carolers left the Golden Living Center, we traveled a short distance to another nursing home, again one that Steve and I had checked out and rejected. As we entered, an elderly man sitting in his wheelchair in the hall raised his hand in greeting to us. One of our youngsters hurried forward and gave him a handmade Christmas card. The old man took the card and gave the boy a smile.

I stared at the old man. His dignified pose, his well-groomed person, and, most of all, his attitude of greeting life as it walked into the door, reminded me so much of John. I didn't see age or disability there. I saw love, love of life despite being in circumstances that might have defeated a less appreciative person. I wanted to step up and hug and kiss the old man. I wanted to tell him how much I loved and missed him, but my rational self was in charge. I simply stepped forward, put my hand gently on his shoulder, gave him a smile and said, "Merry Christmas."

"Merry Christmas to you," he said and gave me back a glorious smile.

I was no longer apprehensive about visiting the nursing home where John had been. As it turned out, that particular home was not on our list anyway.

Our caroling turned in a different direction. We visited several homes where members of our congregation were shut-ins. These visits were illuminating, for other than the homes of the members of the bridge club, I had not visited other congregants. I received from these homes a feeling of community, the extension of church into life, rather than the familiar community of praise and worship in church on Sundays. Visiting the sick, filling their homes with joyous Christmas songs, and listening to them sing with us is active worship, the sharing of love that God asks of us.

In our last home, we were still singing, though a little tired, from the exercise of our voices and the tramping in and out of Rosie the Trolley. We were also pleasantly full of cookies provided for us by the mates of our shut-in congregants. Suddenly, we heard a sharp bumping noise, but ignored it, and sang on, albeit with ears poised to hear an explanation. Someone provided one: "Rosie's fallen into a ditch!" We stopped singing.

Somehow the trolley had slipped its parking brake in the hilly driveway and drifted over a curb into a drainage ditch there. A towline was found and a heavy car tried to pull Rosie free, but to no avail. We were stuck, miles from the church parking lot where our cars were awaiting us. Calls were made and relatives or other congregation members came to rescue us. We drove away, leaving behind the pastor, Rosie's driver, who is a member of our congregation, and some of the carolers who wanted to see the outcome of, not one, but the two towing trucks it took to lift, tug and push Rosie back into service.

Rosie's less than graceful exit from our lives that night brought me back to my present life. I was cold, sleepy, and ready to go home. Yet, when I got back in my house, the caroling lingered. The music of the evening had so nurtured me that I still felt like singing. The impact of the experience reminded me of a movie I had seen; *The Singing Revolution* is a documentary about the small nation of Estonia that freed itself from the tyranny of Soviet occupation by a revolution, not of guns, but of the clever use of their national pastime, singing. What power song has!

The singing of the Christmas carols was equally powerful for me. I felt the same kind of healing with music that I had experienced earlier on my trip to the Mediterranean. No matter what was in store for me, I knew that all would be well. Perhaps the nursing home residents and the shut-ins we had visited felt that healing power in our songs as well. I hoped so.

Chapter Fifteen:
A Certain Conclusion
(2010)

I was eight years old when I had my first conscious experience with death. I lay in the crib my mother had set up in the dining room when my younger sister Flo first got sick with scarlet fever. Flo recovered, but three weeks later it was my turn.

I remember, in the delirium, feeling like I was a pile of bones all, incongruently, tied in a tangle so that there was nothing of me but a round blob of young bones. How curious, I thought. I wasn't afraid, just curious. Then the blob was gone, and all seemed empty; yet the emptiness was gray, a something rather than nothing.

Slowly, I became aware of the door in the dining room, the one that led to the outside and had a four-paned window in it. In the window a figure appeared. It was Mrs. Crocker. I was so happy to see the neighbor woman I dearly loved. When I played with her daughter Margaret, I'd often go to their house and eat doughnuts, store-bought doughnuts, the fluffy kind with powdered sugar that melts into

sweetness on the tongue. Mom would never buy doughnuts, let alone allow me to eat them. She made her own
version of doughnuts out of homemade bread dough, and,
though she sprinkled those fried goodies with powdered
sugar, the taste was of sturdy bread not the squishy texture
of sweetness I craved.

I loved the informality of Mrs. Crocker's household
where she always seem to have time to be with us, not like
our mother who had to do the washing, the baking, the
cooking, the sewing, anything other than playing with us.

Now in the grayness following my delirium, Mrs.
Crocker was there, her dark hair pulled back from her high
forehead, her clothes strangely dark grey. She said nothing.
I knew that she was dead. I remember being told that she
had died, yet here she was standing before me, the only
barrier between us being the dining room door, the single
object in the whole room that retained its reality.

In the lower pane of the dining room door window, I
saw Mrs. Crocker raise her hand and, with it, gesture for me
to come with her. I wanted to go. I trusted her, and I knew
that where she was I would be happy, but I shook my head.

"I'm sorry," I said. "I can't go with you. My Mommy and
Daddy need me."

The room suddenly filled with daylight. There was no
one behind the glass of the dining room door window. I was
in the crib, looking up at my weeping mother and I said to
her, "Can I have some pineapple juice?"

My mother put her hand on my forehead. "Thank God,"
she said, and then to me, "Of course, of course you can
have pineapple juice and maybe a little chicken soup?" I
nodded. I was hungry.

My miraculous recovery from scarlet fever became a
favorite story of my mother's. "I got so excited," she'd tell
her listeners in the years that followed, "that I poured the
chicken soup in the glass and put the pineapple juice in

a bowl! I had prayed. I had prayed so hard that night. I threw out the doctor's medicine and gave her Humphrey's Number 1 every hour." Humphrey's medications were homeopathic, not necessarily endorsed by physicians who had their own mysterious concoctions of remedies in the black medical bag carried in their house calls. Antibiotics for serious illness came into general use only after World War II.

I didn't tell my mother about seeing Mrs. Crocker. I didn't want her to feel badly that I wanted to go with her. Besides, having my mother's joy and undivided attention felt really good to me—though I wrinkled my nose at the first taste of cold chicken soup in a juice glass. Nor did I identify my experience as one of nearly dying until I read Raymond Moody's *Life After Life*, published in 1975. It was Dr. Moody who coined the phrase "near-death experience."

My mother lost her first-born child Raymond to scarlet fever when he was twenty-four months old. She talked of Raymond's death all her life. "Everything I love dies," she used to tell me, indicating that if she didn't love us, her surviving children, or least *didn't say* she loved us, we would not die as Raymond had. No wonder she was so scared when she thought I, too, would die of the disease that took her only son.

Even if she superstitiously avoided showing her love for us openly, Mom expressed her love by taking very good physical care of her children: seeing that we had enough to eat and clothes to wear; nursing us when we were sick; and arguing with Dad that we needed to be educated. Girls, born in the early nineteen twenties and thirties, were generally viewed as potential housewives, even by most fathers. Mom, an early feminist in her attitudes, wanted more for her girls.

Mom had a near-death experience of her own, in her thirties, when she had trouble coming out of anesthesia after all her remaining teeth were pulled, a common practice in early twentieth century dentistry. "They kept calling me to come back," she'd relate in her story to anyone who'd listen. "I didn't want to. I got up to the gates of heaven; they opened wide, and Raymond came running toward me with his little arms outstretched." She'd pause and then continue with a hint of awe in her voice, "The dentist said to me that my heart stopped beating. He was afraid I wouldn't return."

We have odd notions of death. We act as if we have control over it, and we do to some extent. With modern medicine, we postpone dying. Prayer, too, seems to work, as it did with my older sister Marion when she suffered a series of broken bones, infection, and a seizure that put her in a Hospice facility. She recovered from that experience, eventually returning to life in her own home.

There is within us a strong will to live. Maybe that tenacity makes it hard to even contemplate our own deaths. Yet, as we age and draw nearer to our own demise, we find ourselves making peace with the idea. For some, it is a compromised peace. Others seem content to accept the reality of death, especially if they have a strong belief in an afterlife. I'm not sure what to think about death although I am one that has a strong belief in an afterlife.

In a second Bible class—this one on Incarnation—I am once more a teaching assistant to Pastor Tim. We talk about death, not in the actual process of dying, but in the sense of what we believe about death. In the first session of this class I was surprised when my classmates consistently offered views of a physical resurrection of the human body. Even though the belief in a resurrected body is one we state on Sundays when we say the Apostle's Creed in church, for me, I envision a spiritual body, not a physical one, as the resurrected being.

The night after the first class I experienced a dream in which I was writing a story called *Five Minutes Later.* The dream was obviously triggered by Tim's assignment to write what would happen to us five minutes after we died. The commentary I wrote for this class was the story I was writing in that dream. It begins:

"Oh my God!"

"Yes." His voice was filled with love and welcome, drawing me in with its certainty, its reassurance that I was indeed in the right place and that, overwhelming as it was, I could trust the ecstasy that seemed to be my new being.

"The colors! I have never seen vibrancy, such an array of brilliance, such, oh I don't know, such indescribable beauty!"

He smiled and in His face I saw a soft glowing light that combined the colors around and within us. I was filled with the warmth of that light and knew that, at last, that warmth, that ultimate love in the light, was enough. My body was of a spiritual essence that seemed more alive than I had ever been, more freely available, more capable, yet utterly devoid of desire.

In the rest of the story I walk and talk with Jesus in the way I've sung such meetings in countless church hymns, so I know, rationally, that my experience, dream or not, is in line with all that I have learned and felt during my lifetime. Yet, I find the story compelling; it seems as if it were presented as a gift to me, a glimpse of what an afterlife may actually be.

In a later writing for this same class, I describe Heaven. "My fantasy of a heaven is one of a freed spirit, able to nestle entirely with God and lose all that is described as self—to reunite with my Creator and have no need, anymore, to be unique."

I can't imagine writing words like these in my youth. The business of youth is to live as fully as one can in the expectation of building a fine future. As I age, I know that life is limited. The building of my future has mostly been accomplished, so my business, now, is to strengthen my faith so that I can let go of my life when my time comes.

I've never seen anyone actually die. I was with John as he was dying, but his last breath came in the early morning hours when I was asleep. The telephone woke me.

"Mr. Palmer expired at three-twenty this morning," the voice said. I was calm.

"What now?" I asked.

"You can come down and be with him before I call the funeral home," she said.

I woke the family. His daughter Cathy and her husband Randy were sleeping in my guest room. Joya and Maura, adult granddaughters, were on the living room couch. We were all talking at once, trying to comprehend what had happened. The nursing home doctor had said John wouldn't die for a few days more. I had no answers—I didn't even want to hear the questions. All I wanted was to be there with John.

I rushed back into my room, threw on clothes, and headed for my car.

"Wait, wait," Cathy called, but I wouldn't wait. I needed to be there. "Let her go," I heard Randy say.

Driving through the cold, dark, wintry morning I fought the urge to burst into tears. *Drive, concentrate on driving,* I told myself. We passed the place where John had first been in rehab. We? I felt a "we" in the car. I'm not sure what that feeling was all about, only that I knew something as significant as John's death didn't come alone.

I arrived at the nursing home and rang the doorbell. The nurse on duty let me in and then left me to stride the long empty hallway by myself. I couldn't hear my footsteps. I felt as if I were floating.

There he was on his bed, lying still, peaceful in his hospital nightgown. A very pleased smile was on his face. I leaned over and kissed him. He was still warm, blessedly still warm. I said my goodbyes then, telling him how glad I was that he was safely home. I told him I loved him and I held his hand. No response of course.

His son Michael came in then, followed soon after by the rest of the family. They gathered around him, touching him, kissing him, saying goodbye. They clipped locks of his hair to take in remembrance and asked me if I wanted some. I didn't. I knew I needed nothing to remember John in death; he had given me all that I needed in life.

I am drawn in my reading to books that describe near-death experiences or explain with a certain degree of authority what life after death is like. Because I am educated, I take what I read with a healthy dose of skepticism. No one really knows what an afterlife is. I believe that no one knows, yet I can state with the certainty of faith that an afterlife exists, an assurance I especially feel when someone I love dies.

Beyond a will and instructions written to my younger son, I have made no special preparation for my own death. Some of my friends have pre-paid for their funerals and bought cemetery plots. I haven't felt the need to make my son Steve's job of seeing to my funeral an easy task for I know that making decisions after someone dies reaffirms life. There is something left to do for the loved one, and doing something often brings comfort.

When I was studying for a degree in community counseling, my professor required that we students visit a psychic to experience another kind of counseling. He knew and trusted the psychic he had chosen for us. Ruth Simon was not only a psychic, but also a medium. During the reading, my father came through to us.

I was startled when Ruth told me, "There is someone here. He's holding his throat."

Immediately, I thought of my father, who had been successfully treated for throat cancer. "That can't be Dad," I said, "he died of a stroke."

"It is your father," she said. He is holding up three fingers." I froze. "No, I said. No. Two fingers."

I was living in Hawaii when my father died in Maryland. Just a little over a month earlier I had visited with him. I was divorcing my first husband, whom my father loved, and he was upset with me. We had an argument of sorts over my decision, which, in his eyes, I had compounded by bringing with me, to the family home, a younger man; Ted eventually became my second husband. I was a year sober, and, in a very clumsy way, I was trying to make amends to my father, for I had also upset him, in my drinking days, by making emotional and incomprehensible phone calls to him.

Dad thought me unstable. He couldn't understand why I was divorcing Bud or how I would manage to support the family without a husband. He wanted me to leave my children with him so that he and Mom could raise them. They were nearly eighty at this point.

"No, Dad," I said. "I deeply appreciate all that you have done for me in my life, but I'm sober now. I am forty years old, and I'm in charge of my own life."

Dad was old, sick and visibly weary.

"I'm sorry I have disappointed you," I said, "I've been very sick myself, but I am well, now, and you can trust me."

He looked at me with sad eyes.

"You know the trouble is, Dad, that we have always loved each other too much."

He got up from his chair and opened wide his arms. Relieved, I stepped into his welcome embrace. "Let just forget this," he said, confirming the strength of the bond between us. We set aside all differences for the rest of my stay.

I went back to Hawaii. Very soon after my visit, Dad was hospitalized with another stroke. I sent him a card with just my name signed to it. I couldn't shake the feeling of the last argument we had, so I didn't write "love" on the card.

Flo called, and told me Dad was hurt because I didn't sign the card with love, so I sat down and wrote a long letter telling him not to be afraid of dying. I assured him that he had been a good father to us, citing specific ways in which he had nurtured and cared for us, telling him I knew he had done the best he could. I loved him dearly, I told him. When I finished, I got into my car, drove to the post office and mailed the letter. It was too late. He died before it arrived.

Because I was too emotionally fragile, I didn't attend my father's funeral. Dad died early in October, less than a month after my divorce was final and a little less than two months after my intense visit with him. I was alone with my children. (Ted, having served his time in the Navy, was in his hometown of Chicago, trying to decide whether to stay there or come back to me; he wasn't sure he wanted to live in Hawaii.) Besides, I was afraid if I went to Dad's funeral, my younger sister might confront me for withholding my love from my father as he was dying. I had more stress than I could handle; I needed to stay close to the support of my hometown twelve-step groups. Mom told me later she burned my letter, unopened, on Dad's grave.

In describing his last hours in the hospital, Flo told me in a telephone conversation that since I wasn't there, she had reassured our father that he still had herself and our older sister Marion with him. He was not able to speak, Flo said, but held up two fingers, indicating to her the recognition that she and Marion were with him. She did not say what she didn't have to. I felt the weight of not being there.

Now, years later in Hawaii, Ruth, the psychic-medium, told me that the entity she was seeing was holding up three fingers. I protested. "No, no, there's only two!"

"No," she countered. "He's holding up *three* fingers."

"*Dad?*" I said in wonder. "Yes," came the reply. It was the psychic's voice that answered me, but the cadence and the words were my father's.

My tears flowed freely when he said he wrongly mis-judged me in our last talk. He apologized to me and added that he was proud of me.

"What for?" I asked. The psychic explained. "He said a spirit went into the light because of you."

That was too much. I explained to Ruth that once, when I had passed out from drinking, I indeed felt a spirit on my back, holding me down on the bed in which I was lying. I got up and tried to turn on the light at a wall switch and open the door to the bedroom I was in, but the light didn't go on and the doorknob wouldn't turn. The weight of what-ever was on me dragged at me.

"Oh God, help me," I pleaded. The light came on, the door opened, and whatever was on my back slid off.

That spirit, Ruth explained, was one that had not resolved his drinking in his lifetime. "Because the spirit was attached to you, when you got sober, he was able to find sobriety as well."

The story was a stretch for me. It was a nice story and I wanted to believe it, but how could I ever tell anyone about this? Why couldn't I have had a nice chat with my dead father and not be challenged into believing I had some-thing to do with an entity's sobriety, a spirit whom I couldn't possibly have known in life and knew only in a negative way after drinking heavily? Besides, when Ruth told me about the spirit going into the light, it was I who offered her infor-mation about the spirit on my back during that alcoholic episode. My skepticism returned, but I did keep my father's comforting apology with me.

Whether my father came to me or not, and I believe he did, isn't really relevant. What is relevant is that I felt the breech between us healed; I was my father's beloved daughter once more.

Death still is a mystery to me. All I know is that what is left when someone dies is love. The last thing John said to me, before he could no longer talk, was "I love you." Nothing else mattered in that moment.

When I meet with my women friends each Wednesday morning to minister to one another as we grow old together, when I interact with John's family or mine, especially my loyal younger son, when I think of the many friends who came to my aid and did chores and comforted me when I needed help and comfort, and when I pass the peace of the Lord with my church friends, I feel the love we share so freely among us. I even know and feel love in those I've disagreed with and argued with, even in those who have hurt me—for love for me has often motivated their criticism. Love beyond all explanation and understanding is the indestructible essence of life. I know that love survives death, for all the love that was given me, by the ones now gone from this earth, lives in my heart and gives me strength and courage. With all that love, here and beyond, I can face a future that promises an earthly conclusion.

Chapter Sixteen: Awakening to Self (2010)

My car needed a smog certification check-up so I took a theology book with me to read in the car dealer's service area waiting room. There was a man sitting with an opened notebook at the single table, paging through client business sheets. I almost didn't sit at the table, not wishing to intrude, but I also wanted to be able to lay my book on a surface so I could underline passages in it.

I sat down; the man and I exchanged nods.

On the other side of the room, a much younger man was talking loudly on his cell phone, the conversation consisting of irritating banality punctuated with slang phrases of "so's up?" and "cool" and "you know." It was loud idle chatter, and it annoyed us both.

My table companion raised an eyebrow. With a nod in the direction of the young man on the phone, he said loudly, "So rude."

"He sure is," I agreed. "Remember when there were no cell phones to interrupt peace and quiet?"

The man picked up his own phone and smiled. "I've got this (the phone) that will hold all of this (he tapped his notebook), but I'm old-fashioned. I like the security of paper to keep track of my clients."

I smiled. "You don't look so old," I said. Something within me was coaching a closer examination of this man.

"It's the wig," he grinned, pointing to his perfectly coifed hair.

I liked him immediately. His unabashed openness was appealing. "Well, it's a very nice wig," I said.

We began to talk in earnest then, completely forgetting the intrusive cell phone user. I learned that he was 70 years old and was looking for a place to retire. He had a house in an adjoining county that he had put on the market for $900,000 since he no longer needed so much space. He owned his business of installing outdoor lighting for other businesses, and was ambivalent about actually retiring. He didn't want to leave his customers without his personal service. Still, he was looking at retirement communities, and we talked for a while about that, since I live in such a community.

The conversation turned to ethnicity—he was partly Italian (John was all Italian). Seeing my theology book, which had a stark picture of the Cross on it, he volunteered that he was a non-practicing Catholic (John had been too). As we talked religion, attitudes and moral principles, I saw a man who was tolerant of others and had thoughts about ethics and justice similar to my own.

This was getting good. Within me stirred a hope that I just might be looking at someone who could be a companion to me. I felt the sweet glow of a happy mood.

I ventured a query. "What does your wife think of retirement?"

"My wife passed two years ago."

"Oh, I'm sorry," I said. My sympathy was sincere, for I knew the pain of grief. I also was heartened that he was a widower and might be ready for some companionship himself.

"We had 43 years together," he said.

"It can get very lonely," I said.

"Yes. I have a girlfriend who lives with me."

Pop! There went my hope of developing this lovely conversation into something more. Simultaneous with that moment, our customer service representatives came in to tell us our cars were ready.

The man and I shook hands. "Very nice talking to you," we said to one another and off we went to our own lives.

Much to my surprise my happy mood lingered. Although I was unable to have this intriguing man in my life—right age, right financial stability, right attitudes, I felt good. I realized I had made another turn; I had felt a normal, natural attraction to a man and felt his attraction to me. I experienced no anxiety, no ambivalence, and no confusion as I had in considering relationships early in my grief. This present encounter was a pleasant, innocent flirtation with the possibility of developing a new relationship. I realized that I had acted and responded to this man from interest in a particular man rather than in need for someone to love me. I felt healed, whole again, two years and two months after John died.

Maybe the wholeness will last a little while, maybe the rest of my life. In any case I feel alive once more. Aroused from my deep sleep of a woman defined by aging and grief, I have awakened to a world that is mine once more, a world of possibilities and interactions with other humans as perfect and as flawed as I am. I can move out of my loneliness, out of my anxieties, out of my limitations and out of the temptation to hide from the complexities of life. I can move out of these components of suffering into a world that holds love and appreciation for me, real and lasting life qualities for me to feel and own, and, at that same time, share with others.

I have learned so much in my two years of grieving. Life is complex with few easy answers to our dilemmas, yet for most of our lives, we can find reasonable accommodations to our problems if we are able to gain insight and adjust our expectations, attitudes and actions to the realities of our circumstances. For me, an acceptance of what is, rather than a focus on what might have been, is a good starting place. As the Serenity Prayer suggests: accept the things I cannot change, change the things I can, and ask for wisdom to know the difference between the two.

As I worked on rebuilding my life, I gained a greater appreciation of being a finite creature. Moving inexorably towards the end of life is ordinarily an unwelcome awareness for it brings with it fear of the unknown and distress in facing loss. I was obviously grappling with those fears, albeit with some humor and sensitivity, when I wrote the essay "The Stranger in Me" ten years ago. When we are young, we age enthusiastically. We look forward to being old—being old enough, that is, to do whatever we want to do. Aging becomes problematic the moment we start to obsess on being too old. We tend to magnify our limitations whether it's wrinkles in our faces or not being able to move as fast as we used to. In focusing on the limitations of age, we risk losing touch with our lives and may find ourselves living in those limitations instead of concentrating on the intrinsic worth of who we are at any moment of our lives.

Ironically, in these neurotic states we experience the oddity of dying while living. In my case, after John died, hiding in sleep and hours of game playing on the computer, envying relationships my friends had, listlessly attending a lifelong learning class or resisting participation in a church preschool building program are all ways in which I was dying while living.

Learning to trust that each day is sufficient, that we will have what we need for that day's requirements takes the fear out of aging. Getting to that trust takes time and practice. We are so used to being anxious for the future that we habitually forget to live in the present. Moving forward each day into whatever is offered as a daily slice of life is learning to walk in faith.

When we are able to live in trust we begin to resonate with life and life becomes a revelation. "Faith perceives patterns of meaning and direction," Douglas John Hall says in his book, *God and Human Suffering: A Exercise in the Theology of the Cross.* "To speak more accurately, it sees the miraculous!" Hall expands this thesis with the simple, yet astounding truth that these miracles are "true miracles of the everyday sort: the miracle of life going on; the miracle of something and not nothing; the miracle of purpose."

Marking my calendar and then actually going to church a month after John died, I didn't consciously realize I was stepping into a faith that would provide meaning and direction for me. I was only looking for comfort so I didn't see the everyday miracles Hall describes, but they were there for me, nevertheless.

The women of the church who asked me to join their bridge club gave me that "miracle of something" Hall speaks of—that "something" to counter the "nothing" I felt. They gave me the miracle of purpose that supplied some relief to grief, some enjoyment, however brief.

The everyday sort of miracle occurred again when a friend and her son and my son Steve took me to the giant redwoods in Northern California where, among the trees, I found a sense of patience, endurance, and a possibility of life beyond adversity.

Bright-eyed young Chinese girls, whose presence and enthusiasm for life cheered me and moved me in the direction of serving others, were another manifestation of the miraculous for they set me on a pathway towards joy.

Through it all were my friends, Helga, Anne, Myra, and Maureen, who were there for me in our Wednesday group meetings, helping me cope with my sorrow and sharing their problems with me, as well, giving me opportunity to serve them too, and to begin once more to appreciate that I am not alone. In also sharing joys with me, my women friends elicited laughter from me and I felt hope for joys of my own.

These life events are spiritual events. In coming out of myself as the center of the world, even though I must live in consciousness of myself, I can use my gifts to reach out and relate to others and thus experience spiritual growth.

Without faith, miracles aren't easily perceived. Indeed faith itself isn't easily apparent. In my case, faith began to develop significance and strength as I was challenged to face my worse fears. My beloved friends Dom and Pat, struggling with end of life issues, yet encouraging me to live my life fully, revealed an important truth: though our lives are finite, we can continue to serve and love one another even as we die. As if to reinforce this lesson in love, a few days after Dom died, I was faced with the terrifying prospect of losing my beloved sister Marion, while grieving the loss of Dom, and with the simultaneous and sorrow-producing refusal of my younger sister to speak to me. I was challenged indeed!

In these griefs, the other very significant loss in my life—my continuing disconnection with my older son and my grandchildren—surfaced. I profoundly missed the comfort and solace that John would have provided. In my utter helplessness I reached out to Tim, my pastor, who told me to trust in God, and thus began another miracle in my everyday life, the miracle of the power of belief.

In my misery I believed Tim and did as he told me. I put my trust in God, kneeling and praying, through my tears, that God's will be done. An answer came. I need therapy, I thought, so off I went to a therapist where I learned once again to accept with grace, but this time with a greater understanding, that I could not, nor did I need to, mend or change anyone else; I could help myself by loving and forgiving those who may not love or forgive me. As the days and months passed, God answered our prayers for my sister Marion, bringing her out of danger and back to her home. Her recovery is a dynamic manifestation of the love and mercy of God.

Finally, there is the gift of serving my pastor, Tim. By allowing me to plan and teach with him, he opened my world to the use of my intellect once more and the exercise of my skills. Studying the Bible with tools from the works of noted theologians and input from my classmates brought me, at last, to a conscious appreciation of the love, protection and guidance I receive from God.

Into the everyday miracle of which Hall speaks was a very special travel experience for me that involved music. On the cruise ship in the Mediterranean, I was filled with classical music every time our seminar met. On land in the great and ancient Greek amphitheater at Epidaurus, I sang and others joined me. Singing moves us. We open our mouths and sing and we feel something, even if our voices are poor, our spirits are lifted by song, the same lift in spirit I felt in caroling with the church. Great voices or instruments played by talented artists create mood and harmonies that resonate with our spirits. Singing, sighing, dancing, exercising, creating a good meal or great art, or any activity we perceive as joyous brings us in communion with the spirit.

I know and respect the fact that people have their own images, their own perceptions of God, and their own names for a higher power that provides comfort and guidance in life. Even atheists, I believe, have a sense of something beyond human power—some have told me they find that comfort and power in nature. I do not share my experience to influence others to see God as I see God, only to offer my story as a point of identity and hope for those who suffer as I have suffered. I cannot walk another's path for him or her. I can offer to share some room on my path or shine a light on a similar one that is there for the taking.

Still, I know there is within us all a spirit that works to bring us wholeness. Some scholars call this presence *consciousness* and attempt to rigorously examine and study consciousness in intellectual terms. I use the term *spirit* and find an intellectual understanding of spirit eludes me, for spirit exists for me more as feeling rather than thought. Throughout my grieving and recovery, I have been guided by an affirming and loving presence within me that I have learned to recognize as the Holy Spirit. When I opened myself to the experience of God within a church community, I began to intuitively know how to act, how to speak, and how to share my life in a way that brings love to me and elicits love from me.

Grief is not a finite entity. It comes into one's life after a loss and it stays as long as the loss is remembered. I know that I am not done entirely with grieving, even for John, but I also know that I have done the work grief requires and have begun to fashion a new life that brings me a measure of happiness and occasional joy. In moving forward in my life and taking action by going to church, having social contacts with my friends, traveling, and getting involved in the work of the church, I have also found myself feeling younger and invigorated. I've banished the fear and barriers of old age by living in the present and being grateful for what I have. The stranger within me has become a friend.

About the Author

Kay Mehl Miller worked as a journalist for a daily newspaper and wrote freelance feature stories for *The Baltimore Sun* while in college. Later in life, she became a columnist and reporter for various alternative lifestyle print and online media. She taught school in Hawaii, and after receiving a Master of Education, Counseling and Guidance degree from the University of Hawaii, she opened a private practice in psychotherapy. At the age of 58, Kay earned her Ph.D. in psychology from Saybrook University.

Kay is also the author of *Talking It Over: Understanding Sexual Diversity*.